THE EMPATHY MACHINE: AI AND THE NEW AGE OF CONNECTION

HOW ARTIFICIAL INTELLIGENCE IS REDEFINING RELATIONSHIPS, TRUST, AND HUMAN CONNECTION IN THE DIGITAL ERA

MICHAEL FINK

INTRODUCTION

The Empathy Machine: AI and the New Age of Connection is more than just a book—it's a call to understand the shifting dynamics of how we relate, trust, and connect in a world increasingly shaped by artificial intelligence.

When I first started researching the concept of AI-powered empathy, I was struck by one profound question: *Can machines truly care?* This book doesn't just answer that —it dives deep into the promise, pitfalls, and potential of emotional AI. From virtual therapists to customer service bots that "feel," this is about the fascinating ways machines are stepping into emotional spaces once reserved for humans.

This journey isn't just for tech enthusiasts; it's for anyone curious about where humanity is headed. I'll be your guide, balancing high-level ideas with practical insights, real-world examples, and pro secrets to keep things not only informative but transformative.

Goals for Readers

- **Understand** the science and philosophy behind empathetic AI.
- **Discover** real-world applications revolutionizing industries like healthcare, education, and entertainment.
- **Analyze** the ethical and cultural questions AI evokes.
- **Apply** insights to navigate an AI-driven world with clarity and confidence.
- **Envision** the future of human connection in a hybrid world of empathy-driven technology.

CHAPTER 1: THE BIRTH OF THE EMPATHY MACHINE

A rtificial Intelligence (AI) is often described as a tool of logic and computation, but its evolution into the realm of emotions—empathy, understanding, and connection—marks a defining moment in human history. Emotional AI, or empathetic machines, has transitioned from conceptual experiments to real-world applications, fundamentally reshaping how we perceive technology's role in our lives. This chapter explores the origins, milestones, and transformative potential of empathetic AI, weaving in compelling examples and expert insights.

The Roots of Emotional AI

The journey of empathetic AI began with a simple idea: What if machines could replicate human understanding? In the mid-20th century, computer scientists started exploring how computers could mimic natural human conversation.

One of the earliest milestones was **ELIZA**, created in the 1960s by Joseph Weizenbaum at MIT. ELIZA simulated the behavior of a psychotherapist, responding to users' statements with questions or affirmations. For instance:

- **User:** "I feel sad today."
- **ELIZA:** "Why do you feel sad today?"

While ELIZA's responses were formulaic, users often found them comforting. The program didn't understand emotions, but it highlighted something fascinating: humans project their own feelings onto machines when they appear empathetic.

Fast forward to the 21st century, the arrival of **Apple's Siri** (2011) marked a pivotal shift. Siri brought AI into everyday life with personality, humor, and conversational abilities. While Siri's main function was productivity—setting reminders, providing directions, or answering trivia—it also entertained with witty replies. Siri hinted at the possibilities of making AI relatable, an essential step toward empathy-driven technology.

In the late 2010s and beyond, advancements in deep learning and natural language processing led to transformative tools like **GPT-3** (the predecessor of tools like ChatGPT). GPT-powered systems can analyze nuanced emotional cues, tailoring responses to simulate empathy. For example, they can respond to a stressed user with words of encouragement or offer actionable advice in moments of uncertainty.

Milestones in the Evolution of Emotional AI
1. ELIZA: A Simple Start with a Profound Impact
- Developed in 1966, ELIZA used pattern matching to emulate conversation.
- While its approach was basic, it revealed how humans interact emotionally with machines.
- *Key Takeaway*: Even rudimentary empathy simulations can establish a sense of connection.

2. Siri and the Era of Relatable AI

• Apple's Siri combined functionality with personality, setting a new standard for voice assistants.

• Siri's ability to respond with humor or empathy made it feel more human, despite its limitations.

• *Key Takeaway*: Personality can make even task-oriented AI feel approachable.

3. Deep Learning and GPT-Powered Tools

• With advanced algorithms, tools like ChatGPT analyze emotional cues to respond empathetically.

• Applications include mental health support, customer service, and creative collaboration.

• *Key Takeaway*: Empathy in AI relies on adaptability and contextual understanding.

THE PSYCHOLOGY BEHIND Emotional AI

Why do humans respond to machines that appear empathetic? This phenomenon, often called *anthropomorphism*, occurs when people attribute human-like qualities to non-human entities. Emotional AI exploits this by mimicking empathetic behaviors, creating a sense of connection.

Key Psychological Drivers

• **Relatability**: AI's ability to mirror emotions helps users feel understood.

• **Trust**: Empathy builds trust, making users more likely to engage with AI.

• **Emotional Safety**: AI offers a nonjudgmental outlet for expressing feelings.

THREE EXPERT EXAMPLES of Emotional AI in Action

Example 1: ELIZA's Enduring Legacy

ELIZA, despite its simplicity, inspired decades of innovation in conversational AI. Its basic ability to reframe user input—"Tell me more about that"—proved powerful in fostering engagement. Psychotherapists later critiqued it as a superficial imitation, but it paved the way for more advanced systems.

Example 2: Woebot—AI for Mental Health

Modern tools like Woebot, a chatbot for mental health, expand on ELIZA's foundation. Woebot uses cognitive-behavioral therapy techniques to guide users through anxiety or depression.

• *Real-World Scenario*: A user struggling with insomnia receives tailored advice, such as relaxation techniques, based on their responses.

• *Lesson*: Emotional AI doesn't replace therapists but can supplement care with accessible support.

Example 3: GPT-Powered Customer Engagement

Brands like Zendesk use AI chatbots to address customer concerns empathetically. For instance, when a customer expresses frustration, the AI can de-escalate the situation with understanding and solutions.

• *Real-World Scenario*: "I'm really upset about my order being late." → "I understand how frustrating delays can be. Let me prioritize this for you right away."

• *Lesson*: Empathy in business fosters loyalty and improves user satisfaction.

Pro Secrets for Building Empathetic AI

1. Start with Core Human Needs

Focus on designing AI that addresses fundamental emotional needs—validation, understanding, and support.

• *Tip*: Simplicity often outperforms complexity when fostering emotional engagement.

2. Leverage Context for Deeper Connection

AI should analyze contextual cues to tailor responses.

• *Example*: A stressed user might appreciate calm, reassuring language, while a curious user seeks detailed answers.

3. Iterate with Real Feedback

Continuously refine AI based on user interactions.

• *Tip*: Collect feedback on how well the AI simulates empathy and adapt algorithms accordingly.

4. Transparency Builds Trust

Be honest about AI's capabilities and limitations. Users value clarity over unrealistic promises.

• *Example*: Clearly label AI responses to avoid misrepresentation.

5. Balance Relatability with Functionality

Empathy should enhance usability, not overshadow it.

• *Tip*: Prioritize seamless functionality alongside emotional resonance.

THE BIRTH of a Paradigm Shift

The birth of the empathy machine represents more than just technological innovation; it signals a paradigm shift in how we relate to the world around us. Machines once designed solely for efficiency are now being built to connect, inspire, and understand.

As we explore the next chapters, we'll delve deeper into the dynamics of empathy in AI, from its scientific foundations to its societal implications. Let's journey into the heart of what it means for technology to care—and what that reveals about humanity itself.

CHAPTER 2: WHAT MAKES EMPATHY HUMAN?

E mpathy is a cornerstone of human relationships, enabling us to understand, share, and respond to the emotions of others. But what exactly makes empathy human? This chapter explores the core components of empathy, how they operate in humans, and the challenges AI faces in replicating these deeply emotional and relational processes.

Defining Human Empathy

At its essence, empathy is the ability to step into someone else's shoes—feeling and understanding their emotions while responding in a meaningful way. Empathy in humans involves two key dimensions:

1 **Cognitive Empathy**: Understanding another person's emotions or thoughts without necessarily feeling them yourself. For example, knowing why a friend might be upset after losing their job.

2 **Affective Empathy**: Sharing the emotional experience

of another person. If your friend is grieving, you feel their sadness alongside them.

Together, these dimensions form a complete empathetic response, connecting thought, emotion, and action.

CORE ELEMENTS of Human Empathy

1. Emotional Awareness

Humans are deeply attuned to recognizing and interpreting emotions in others through verbal cues, body language, tone, and even subtle facial expressions.

- **Example:** Imagine watching a close friend's face turn from joy to disappointment—you immediately recognize the shift and feel compelled to respond.

2. Perspective-Taking

A critical component of empathy is the ability to see the world from another's viewpoint. This requires imagination, understanding, and a suspension of judgment.

- **Example:** A teacher empathizing with a struggling student considers the challenges the student might be facing at home.

3. Emotional Regulation

Empathy requires balancing your emotional response to avoid becoming overwhelmed or reactive.

- **Example:** A doctor delivering difficult news to a patient must convey compassion without being consumed by emotion.

4. Actionable Response

True empathy doesn't stop at understanding; it often involves taking supportive or compassionate action.

- **Example:** After recognizing a colleague's stress, offering to help with their workload shows empathy in action.

. . .

How AI Replicates Empathy

AI systems attempt to mimic these elements of human empathy by combining data analysis, natural language processing, and predictive algorithms. While machines lack true emotional experiences, they simulate empathetic responses through structured frameworks:

1. Emotional Recognition

Using facial recognition, sentiment analysis, and tone detection, AI systems identify emotions with impressive accuracy.

• **Example:** A virtual customer service agent detects frustration in a user's text or voice and adjusts its tone to appear more understanding: "I see you're upset. Let me help resolve this quickly."

2. Contextual Understanding

AI analyzes context to predict emotional states and craft relevant responses. Machine learning models use large datasets to refine their ability to anticipate human needs.

• **Example:** A health app like Woebot offers personalized mental health exercises based on patterns in a user's interactions.

3. Adaptive Communication

Advanced AI tools like GPT-4 simulate empathetic conversation by adapting their language to match the user's emotional tone.

• **Example:** A user expressing anxiety might receive calming, encouraging language: "I understand this is stressful. Let's explore steps to help ease your mind."

Challenges in AI Replicating Human Empathy

While AI can simulate empathy, its efforts remain fundamentally limited by several factors:

1 Lack of Genuine Emotion

Machines don't feel—they calculate. This limitation can lead to mismatched responses or a lack of genuine warmth that humans naturally provide.

2 Cultural and Contextual Nuance

AI struggles with the subtleties of cultural differences, which can lead to inappropriate or tone-deaf responses.

3 Ethical Concerns

Simulating empathy in AI raises questions: Are users being manipulated by machines designed to "care"? Transparency about AI's capabilities is critical.

THREE EXPERT EXAMPLES of AI Replicating Empathy

Example 1: Replika—AI Companionship

Replika is an AI chatbot designed to simulate friendship. It uses emotional cues from users to craft responses that feel understanding and supportive.

• **Scenario:** A user shares feelings of loneliness, and Replika responds with empathy: "I'm sorry you're feeling this way. I'm here to talk."

• **Lesson:** While comforting, these interactions can feel superficial over time because the AI lacks genuine emotional engagement.

Example 2: Virtual Crisis Counselors

AI-powered crisis support tools, like those used by Crisis Text Line, analyze language patterns to detect distress signals. These tools escalate high-risk conversations to human counselors while offering empathetic AI responses in the meantime.

• **Scenario:** A user texts, "I feel hopeless." The AI

responds: "I'm so sorry you're feeling this way. Let's figure this out together."

- **Lesson:** AI provides initial empathy, but human involvement is crucial for nuanced care.

Example 3: Customer Support with Zendesk AI

AI bots in customer service detect frustration in a customer's tone and adapt their language accordingly.

- **Scenario:** A user types, "I'm so annoyed with this delay!" The bot replies: "I understand how frustrating delays can be. Let me resolve this for you right now."

- **Lesson:** Empathy-driven customer service improves satisfaction and loyalty.

PRO TIPS for Developing Empathy in AI Systems

1 Start with Emotional Awareness

Ensure AI systems are equipped with advanced emotional recognition tools to detect and analyze emotions accurately.

2 Focus on Contextual Understanding

Empathy isn't one-size-fits-all. Train AI to consider cultural, linguistic, and individual nuances.

3 Incorporate Human Oversight

Blend human empathy with AI capabilities to ensure responses are meaningful and ethical.

4 Prioritize Transparency

Communicate that AI is simulating empathy and not experiencing emotions. This fosters trust and prevents user disillusionment.

5 Continuously Evolve

Use user feedback to refine the AI's ability to simulate empathy effectively and appropriately.

. . .

THE HEART of the Empathy Machine

Human empathy is complex, dynamic, and deeply emotional. While AI cannot replicate the fullness of human experience, it can complement it in profound ways— offering scalable, accessible tools for emotional connection. As we continue to explore this intersection of humanity and technology, the question isn't just *how* AI can replicate empathy but how it can deepen and enhance our understanding of ourselves.

CHAPTER 3: THE SCIENCE BEHIND ARTIFICIAL EMPATHY

A rtificial empathy, or emotional AI, hinges on advanced technologies like **machine learning**, **deep learning**, and **neural networks** to simulate human-like understanding and response. Although machines don't possess emotions in the traditional sense, their ability to process, analyze, and replicate emotional cues is nothing short of revolutionary. In this chapter, we'll explore the science behind artificial empathy, including how algorithms are designed to detect, understand, and respond to human emotions.

THE MECHANICS OF EMOTIONAL AI: A Foundation in Algorithms

At the core of emotional AI is a deep understanding of human emotions, which is captured and interpreted through sophisticated algorithms. These algorithms process vast amounts of data, enabling AI systems to simulate human-like empathy in ways that can often seem indistinguishable from true emotional understanding. But how do they do this?

1 Emotion Recognition Algorithms

AI systems are able to recognize emotions through data processing—mainly in the form of **speech**, **text**, and **facial expressions**. To do this, AI systems analyze certain patterns that correspond with emotional states. For instance, the tone of voice, pitch, and tempo in speech can reveal a speaker's emotional state. Similarly, facial recognition algorithms analyze facial expressions, mapping them to specific emotions like happiness, anger, or sadness.

○ **Example:** A tool like **IBM Watson Tone Analyzer** uses natural language processing (NLP) to analyze text and detect emotional tones such as joy, anger, or fear. By evaluating sentence structure, word choices, and context, the AI can infer the emotional state of the user.

○ *Pro Tip*: For AI to accurately replicate empathy, it must be able to integrate both cognitive and emotional signals from multiple sources (e.g., speech and text).

2 Text Analysis and Sentiment Detection

In the realm of text analysis, emotional AI goes a step further by detecting sentiment in written language. Sentiment analysis involves determining the emotional tone behind a sequence of words, whether positive, negative, or neutral. AI can be trained to recognize subtle shifts in sentiment, even down to a word or phrase that carries deep emotional weight.

○ **Example:** A company like **Sentiment140** allows businesses to monitor social media for emotional tone, enabling them to detect how customers feel about their brand or product.

○ *Pro Tip*: When building a customer service AI, you can

train it to recognize distress in customers' language and proactively offer empathy-based responses.

The Role of Neural Networks in Emotional AI

Neural networks are the backbone of deep learning models that power modern AI. These networks consist of layers of nodes (neurons) that process and learn from data in ways that mimic the human brain. Each layer of the network performs a specific function—much like different areas of the brain specialize in different cognitive functions.

1. Recurrent Neural Networks (RNNs)

RNNs are especially useful for emotional AI because they can analyze sequences of data, such as sentences, and retain contextual information over time. For instance, when an AI analyzes a conversation, it needs to remember previous exchanges to correctly interpret emotional shifts and context.

• **Example: Google's BERT (Bidirectional Encoder Representations from Transformers)** uses RNNs to understand the context of words based on the surrounding text. This allows the AI to capture the nuances of emotion that a single sentence might contain.

• *Pro Tip*: If you are designing an AI for long-form conversations (e.g., therapy or support), using RNNs ensures that the system can follow emotional arcs, adapting its responses to ongoing emotional states.

2. Convolutional Neural Networks (CNNs)

CNNs are often used for image recognition, but they also play a role in emotion detection from facial expressions. Through layers of filtering, CNNs identify key facial landmarks—such as the curvature of the mouth or the openness of the eyes—that are indicative of specific emotions.

• **Example: Face++** uses CNNs to analyze facial expressions and predict emotions, providing real-time feedback on a person's emotional state.

• *Pro Tip*: By incorporating CNNs, an AI system can recognize non-verbal emotional cues and respond with empathy, offering personalized responses based on facial expressions.

3. Generative Adversarial Networks (GANs)

GANs are used for generating synthetic data, such as images or even text. These networks can be used to create emotionally resonant content, enhancing the empathy response of AI systems. GANs have been leveraged in AI-generated art and text to evoke emotional reactions from users.

• **Example: Artbreeder** uses GANs to create emotionally charged artworks based on user input, allowing for personalized emotional experiences in digital formats.

• *Pro Tip*: GANs can be used in empathetic AI to create emotionally appropriate responses or interactions based on user data, ensuring that the AI's reply resonates emotionally with the user.

How AI Learns Empathy: Training Data and Supervised Learning

Like any machine learning model, emotional AI relies heavily on data for training. But it's not just any data—emotional AI requires carefully curated datasets that reflect real human emotions. This process involves **supervised learning**, where AI is trained on large datasets with labeled emotional data, such as:

• **Labeled facial expressions**: Annotated images showing emotional states.

- **Voice tone**: Audio recordings labeled with the emotional context (e.g., happy, sad, frustrated).
- **Textual sentiment**: Large datasets of text labeled by human annotators to reflect the emotional tone.

Supervised Learning and Fine-Tuning

During the supervised learning phase, an AI is shown examples of human emotions and their corresponding responses. The AI's algorithms are then adjusted to ensure that when it encounters a similar situation, it can respond appropriately. This fine-tuning process is essential to improving the empathy that the AI can express.

- **Example: Woebot**, an AI chatbot for mental health, uses supervised learning to refine its responses based on real conversations with users. It's trained to recognize subtle emotional shifts, adapting its responses to provide the most empathetic reaction possible.
- *Pro Tip*: The key to successful empathetic AI is ongoing training and adjustment. As more data is collected, the AI can become more attuned to emotional nuances.

CHALLENGES IN EMOTION **Recognition and AI Limitations**

Despite these advances, emotional AI faces several challenges:

1 **Contextual Ambiguity**

Emotions are complex and often depend on a range of factors, from personal history to cultural background. AI struggles to understand these subtleties, sometimes offering responses that seem disconnected from the user's real emotional state.

2 **Ethical Implications**

As AI systems grow more capable of simulating empathy, ethical concerns arise. For instance, is it ethical for a machine to pretend to care, especially in sensitive areas like mental health? Transparency and user consent are critical.

3 Cultural Sensitivity

AI often struggles with understanding cultural context and differences in emotional expression. For example, direct expressions of emotion in some cultures may be viewed as impolite, whereas others may value open emotional expression. Ensuring that AI systems are culturally aware is a major hurdle.

PRO TIPS for Designing Emotionally Intelligent AI Systems

1 Use Diverse Datasets

To ensure that AI systems respond empathetically across various cultural contexts, use diverse datasets that include multiple emotional expressions and cultural perspectives.

2 Ensure Contextual Awareness

Build AI systems that consider both verbal and non-verbal cues for a more accurate reading of the user's emotional state.

3 Improve Real-Time Feedback

Implement real-time machine learning techniques to allow the AI to continuously adapt and improve its emotional responses based on user interactions.

4 Prioritize Ethical Standards

Communicate to users that AI is simulating empathy, not feeling it. Maintain transparency around the system's capabilities and limitations.

5 Promote Continuous Human Oversight

For sensitive applications, ensure that human oversight is integrated into AI systems to provide a balance between artificial and human empathy.

. . .

The Future of Empathetic AI

The scientific foundations behind artificial empathy are only the beginning. As we refine neural networks, sentiment analysis tools, and facial recognition software, AI's ability to simulate empathy will only grow more sophisticated. But even as AI becomes more emotionally intelligent, it's crucial to remember that empathy, at its core, is deeply human—a complex, multi-layered experience that machines can only approximate, not truly replicate.

CHAPTER 4: REAL-WORLD APPLICATIONS OF EMPATHETIC AI

As artificial intelligence continues to evolve, its potential for fostering deeper human connections has been explored in several real-world sectors. Healthcare, customer service, and education are just a few of the areas where empathetic AI is having a profound impact. By simulating emotional understanding, AI systems are not only transforming these industries but also enhancing the quality of interactions between people and machines.

1. Healthcare: Enhancing Patient Care with Empathy

In healthcare, the importance of empathy in patient care cannot be overstated. Patients who feel understood and supported are more likely to adhere to treatment plans and experience positive outcomes. However, healthcare professionals are often pressed for time and overwhelmed by administrative tasks, which can make it difficult to maintain the level of emotional connection that patients need. This is where AI-driven solutions can make a difference.

Examples:

• **Woebot Health:** This AI-powered chatbot is designed to help individuals with mental health concerns. It uses cognitive behavioral therapy (CBT) principles to engage users in therapeutic conversations. Woebot can detect signs of distress through language and respond empathetically, offering coping strategies and emotional support.

○ *Pro Tip*: Integrating AI into mental health care allows therapists to scale their impact, providing more frequent check-ins and support for patients who might not otherwise have access to regular care.

• **AI for Elderly Care:** In elderly care, AI-powered robots like **Pepper** are being used to interact with patients, detect signs of loneliness, and offer comforting conversations. These robots are equipped with emotional recognition capabilities, responding to facial expressions and voice tone to provide personalized interactions.

○ *Pro Tip*: For elderly patients, AI offers a way to combat social isolation, acting as both a companion and a bridge to human caregivers.

• **AI in Pain Management:** AI tools like **PainChek**, an app used in healthcare settings, help to detect pain in patients who are unable to communicate, such as those with dementia. Using facial recognition algorithms, the app can assess a patient's facial expressions and determine whether they are in pain, helping caregivers provide timely interventions.

○ *Pro Tip*: AI's ability to detect unspoken pain improves patient comfort and ensures more personalized care in situations where verbal communication is limited.

These AI systems are becoming essential in providing emotionally intelligent care, especially in scenarios where human resources are stretched thin. Through continuous learning and feedback, AI systems can adapt to the needs of individual patients, offering more tailored and supportive experiences.

2. Customer Service: Redefining Interaction with Emotional AI

Customer service is an area where AI's ability to simulate empathy is quickly gaining traction. Many companies are using AI to handle routine inquiries, but the next step is ensuring that these systems can respond to customers' emotional needs in real time. AI systems capable of recognizing stress, frustration, or satisfaction can offer a more personalized, empathetic approach to customer support.

Examples:

• **IBM Watson Assistant:** One of the most well-known AI tools in customer service, IBM Watson can be trained to recognize emotional tones in customer queries. For example, if a customer expresses frustration, Watson can adjust its responses to de-escalate the situation and offer empathetic support.

○ *Pro Tip*: To build more empathetic AI customer service agents, ensure the system recognizes both sentiment and context. This enables it to understand why a customer may be upset (e.g., a delayed order or a billing error) and respond accordingly.

• **Chatbots with Emotional Intelligence:** Companies like **LivePerson** have created AI-powered chatbots that not only answer customer queries but also gauge the emotional state of customers during interactions. By tracking sentiment, these bots can provide timely responses that are tailored to the customer's emotional state. For instance, if a customer is angry or upset, the bot might offer a human interaction or suggest immediate solutions to the problem.

○ *Pro Tip*: Emotional AI can greatly enhance customer satisfaction by making interactions feel less transactional and more human, fostering trust and loyalty in your brand.

- **Virtual Assistants in E-Commerce**: AI-powered virtual assistants, like those used by brands such as **H&M**, are being developed to assist customers through the shopping journey. These assistants use empathetic dialogue to make customers feel heard, enhancing their shopping experience. By understanding emotional cues in language, virtual assistants can provide product recommendations, guide users through purchasing, and handle returns—all while maintaining an empathetic tone.

○ *Pro Tip*: Integrate emotional AI into the user experience, offering assistance that feels not only helpful but also compassionate, especially during frustrating moments like checkout issues or shipping delays.

Empathetic AI in customer service improves the quality of interactions and builds a more positive relationship between brands and their customers. It's no longer just about solving problems—it's about fostering a connection.

3. Education: Transforming Learning with Emotional Understanding

The field of education is another area where emotional AI is making waves. Teachers and instructors can use AI to support students not only with academic content but also with emotional and mental well-being. In a world where students are facing increasing pressures, AI can step in to provide personalized, empathetic support, ensuring that learners feel heard, understood, and motivated.

Examples:

• **AI Tutors for Emotional Support**: Tools like **Cerego** and **MATHia** adapt to the learning needs of individual students, offering both academic support and emotional encouragement. When a student struggles with a difficult topic, the AI can detect signs of frustration or anxiety in their responses and provide positive reinforcement or suggest an alternate learning strategy.

○ *Pro Tip*: Emotional AI in education can help students stay engaged by offering encouragement at key moments, preventing feelings of failure or frustration from derailing their learning experience.

• **Emotionally Intelligent Classrooms**: Schools are increasingly integrating AI systems into classrooms to monitor students' emotional states. For example, **AI in Classrooms by Affectiva** tracks facial expressions and body language to gauge students' levels of engagement and emotional reactions. Teachers can then use this data to adjust lessons in real-time, ensuring that students are not just receiving information but are emotionally engaged in the learning process.

○ *Pro Tip*: For teachers, using emotional AI to monitor classroom moods can help identify students who might need additional support—whether it's academic or emotional—before issues become more serious.

• **AI-Driven Mental Health Programs**: Some educational institutions are using AI to support student mental health. Platforms like **Youper** use AI to analyze text input from students, providing them with therapeutic exercises and emotional support. These AI-driven tools use emotional recognition to detect anxiety, stress, or sadness, helping students access mental health resources whenever needed.

○ *Pro Tip*: Implementing AI for mental health support in educational settings allows students to get help without the stigma that can often be associated with seeking therapy, making it more accessible and less intimidating.

In education, emotional AI plays a pivotal role in addressing students' emotional needs while supporting their academic growth. By integrating emotional awareness into learning environments, AI can foster an atmosphere of trust and understanding that helps students thrive.

CHALLENGES AND CONSIDERATIONS in Empathetic AI

While the applications of emotional AI are promising, there are also challenges and ethical considerations that must be addressed.

1 **Privacy Concerns:** In sectors like healthcare and education, where emotional data is highly sensitive, maintaining privacy and data security is critical. It's essential that users are informed about how their data is being used and that proper safeguards are in place to protect it.

2 **Cultural Sensitivity:** As AI systems become more global, they must be designed to recognize cultural differences in emotional expression. What is considered a polite response in one culture may be seen as disengagement in another.

3 **Over-Reliance on AI:** While empathetic AI can greatly enhance human interaction, it should never replace the human element, particularly in areas like mental health care. AI should serve as a tool to augment, not replace, human empathy.

. . .

CONCLUSION: **The Promise of Empathetic AI in the Real World**

As we've seen across healthcare, customer service, and education, empathetic AI is not just a futuristic concept—it's already reshaping industries and improving how we interact with technology. With the ability to simulate empathy, AI is helping us feel heard, understood, and supported in ways that were once thought impossible. The key is ensuring that these systems are deployed responsibly, ethically, and with the emotional intelligence to truly understand and serve human needs.

CHAPTER 5: ETHICS AND EMPATHY: CAN AI CROSS THE MORAL LINE?

As AI continues to evolve and integrate deeper into human lives, one of the most critical concerns arises: **Can AI truly understand and replicate empathy in a morally responsible way?** The ethical implications of creating emotional machines are vast, and we are only beginning to scratch the surface of these dilemmas. While the potential for AI to enhance human experiences is exciting, there are substantial challenges in ensuring that these systems remain ethical, safe, and aligned with human values.

1. Defining Ethical Boundaries in Empathetic AI

When developing AI systems designed to simulate empathy, the question arises: **What moral guidelines should these systems follow?** Unlike human emotions, which are guided by intuition, experience, and culture, AI's emotional responses are algorithmic and based on pre-defined datasets. This disconnect between human emotion and machine learning leads to a fundamental dilemma: **Can AI truly understand the moral nuances of empathy?**

Examples:

• **Emotional Manipulation:** AI's empathetic capabilities could be misused to manipulate users' emotions for profit. A chatbot in customer service, for instance, could exaggerate empathy to sway customers into making decisions they might not otherwise make—such as buying products or services they don't need.

○ *Pro Tip*: Ethical guidelines should be put in place to prevent AI from exploiting human vulnerabilities, especially in sensitive sectors like retail, healthcare, or finance.

• **Unintended Bias:** AI systems are only as ethical as the data they are trained on. If AI models are trained on biased datasets, their empathy simulations can be skewed, leading to unfair or discriminatory outcomes.

○ *Pro Tip*: Ensure that emotional AI systems are trained on diverse, representative data sets, and routinely audit them for bias to guarantee fairness and inclusivity.

• **AI's "Fake" Empathy:** A deeper question about empathetic AI is whether it is ethical to make users believe that machines genuinely care. For instance, chatbots or virtual assistants that engage users emotionally may lead some people to develop attachments, even though these systems lack any true understanding or intent.

○ *Pro Tip*: Transparency is key—users must be made aware that the empathy displayed by AI is not real, and the machine is simply following an algorithm designed to mimic emotional responses.

Creating ethical boundaries for AI that simulate empathy is critical, as these systems could easily cross into areas where human emotions are manipulated or exploited. These challenges make it clear that, while AI can replicate empathy to a degree, it is still far removed from human morality.

2. The Risk of Dehumanization

As AI becomes more adept at simulating empathy, there's a looming concern: **Will these machines replace authentic human connections?** While AI can be a useful tool in supporting emotional well-being, there's a real risk that over-reliance on empathetic machines could erode our need for genuine human interactions. This is particularly concerning in areas like mental health, where the human element is essential to healing.

Examples:

• **AI in Mental Health:** Chatbots like **Woebot** are increasingly being used to support people dealing with anxiety and depression. While these tools provide immediate help and can be a useful supplement to therapy, they are no substitute for the deep, human connection necessary for real healing.

○ *Pro Tip*: Always integrate AI with human oversight, especially in mental health, to ensure that users are getting holistic, well-rounded care, and are not replacing real human relationships with digital substitutes.

• **Social Isolation:** If people start relying more on AI for companionship or emotional support, it could worsen issues like social isolation. For example, AI-powered companions for the elderly, like the **Pepper robot**, are helpful, but they cannot replace the emotional depth and warmth of human relationships.

○ *Pro Tip*: AI should be designed to complement, not replace, human interactions. Creating systems that encourage users to connect with others, or directing them to human resources when necessary, is crucial for preventing isolation.

- **Emotional Dependency**: AI systems could create a false sense of dependency, leading people to rely on machines for emotional validation rather than developing healthy, human relationships.

  o *Pro Tip*: Include features in emotional AI systems that encourage users to engage with real people and seek out human emotional support when necessary.

The danger of dehumanization is one of the most pressing ethical challenges of empathetic AI. While these systems can provide comfort and support, they should never replace the need for real human connection, which is vital for emotional well-being.

3. Manipulating Empathy: Ethical Concerns in Marketing and Advertising

One of the most controversial applications of empathetic AI is its use in marketing and advertising. With its ability to simulate emotions and understand user sentiment, AI has the potential to become a powerful tool for businesses looking to personalize their marketing strategies. However, this presents a significant ethical question: **Should AI be allowed to manipulate human emotions for profit?**

Examples:

- **Emotional Targeting**: AI can be used to analyze social media posts, online behavior, and even facial expressions to create highly targeted advertisements that appeal to a person's emotional state. While this makes for highly effective marketing, it raises concerns about privacy, consent, and the ethics of using AI to influence people's purchasing decisions based on their emotional vulnerabilities.

○ *Pro Tip*: Ensure that AI-driven marketing campaigns are transparent and respect the emotional boundaries of consumers. Always provide users with the option to opt out of personalized ads based on emotional data.

• **Emotional AI in Retail**: Virtual assistants in online shopping platforms can recognize when a customer is frustrated or indecisive and offer empathetic responses to guide them toward a purchase. This can lead to higher conversion rates, but it could also raise ethical concerns about manipulating users into spending more than they intended.

○ *Pro Tip*: Keep the user's best interests at heart by ensuring that emotional AI in retail is used to genuinely enhance the shopping experience rather than coerce customers into purchases.

• **AI-Generated Content**: Social media platforms are increasingly using AI to create emotionally charged content that resonates with users, often triggering strong emotional responses. While this can foster engagement, it can also lead to the spread of misleading information or the manipulation of emotions for political or financial gain.

○ *Pro Tip*: Companies and platforms should ensure that AI-generated content adheres to ethical standards, prioritizing the well-being of users over engagement metrics.

The line between effective marketing and emotional manipulation is thin, and empathetic AI can easily cross it. Businesses must be cautious in their use of emotional AI and always prioritize ethical practices that respect the emotional autonomy of consumers.

4. Accountability and Transparency in Empathetic AI

As AI systems become more integrated into emotional roles, the question of accountability becomes crucial. **Who**

is responsible when an AI system causes harm or acts unethically? If an empathetic AI system makes a mistake, causes emotional distress, or even exploits a user's vulnerability, who is held accountable?

Examples:

• **AI Misinterpretation:** If an AI system misinterprets a user's emotional state and offers an inappropriate response, who is responsible for that error? For instance, an AI therapist might incorrectly diagnose a mental health condition based on incorrect emotional cues.

○ *Pro Tip*: Developers must ensure that emotional AI systems are thoroughly tested for accuracy and that there are clear accountability protocols in place if something goes wrong.

• **Lack of Transparency:** Many AI systems operate as "black boxes," meaning users don't know how decisions are made or what data is being used to influence their experience. This lack of transparency becomes even more concerning when the AI is involved in emotional interactions.

○ *Pro Tip*: Always provide users with clear explanations of how AI systems work, what data is being used, and how their emotional information is being processed.

• **Data Privacy and Consent:** Emotional AI systems often rely on sensitive data, such as facial expressions, voice tone, and even biometric feedback. If this data is mishandled or used without proper consent, it could lead to serious ethical violations.

○ *Pro Tip*: Implement strict data privacy policies, obtain explicit consent from users, and ensure that all data is anonymized and securely stored.

As empathetic AI systems become more complex, accountability and transparency will be paramount in ensuring that these systems are used ethically and responsibly.

5. The Future of Empathetic AI: Ethical Guidelines and the Path Forward

Looking to the future, one of the most critical tasks for developers, policymakers, and society as a whole will be to establish robust ethical guidelines for the development and deployment of empathetic AI. This includes addressing issues of privacy, bias, emotional manipulation, and accountability.

Examples:

• **Ethical AI Frameworks:** Several organizations, such as the **AI Ethics Initiative** and **IEEE**, are working to create ethical frameworks for AI development. These guidelines emphasize transparency, fairness, and accountability.

○ *Pro Tip*: Stay up-to-date on these ethical guidelines and incorporate them into your AI systems from the outset to ensure responsible development.

• **Human-AI Collaboration:** The future of empathetic AI is not one where machines replace humans, but where they collaborate with humans to improve emotional intelligence. This partnership can lead to more emotionally intelligent societies, but only if the right ethical standards are in place.

○ *Pro Tip*: Promote a human-first approach in AI design, where machines are seen as tools that enhance human interactions, not replace them.

• **Public Awareness and Advocacy**: As AI becomes more integrated into everyday life, public education on the ethical implications of AI will be critical. Advocacy groups, regulatory bodies, and AI developers must work together to ensure that the public understands both the potential and the risks of emotional AI.

   ○ *Pro Tip*: Encourage public discourse### Chapter 6: Ethics and Empathy: Can AI Cross the Moral Line?

The rapid advancement of artificial intelligence, particularly in the realm of emotional AI, has opened up new frontiers in human-machine interaction. With AI systems now capable of mimicking empathy, the ethical implications have never been more pressing. How do we define the ethical boundaries of an empathetic machine? Can AI ever truly understand the moral complexities of human emotions, or are we merely creating emotional simulations that, while convincing, still fall short of genuine human understanding?

In this chapter, we will delve into the profound ethical questions surrounding AI's ability to replicate empathy. We will explore the risks of dehumanization, emotional manipulation, and the erosion of trust, and we'll examine how we might set boundaries to ensure that AI remains a force for good, rather than a tool for exploitation.

1. Defining Ethical Boundaries in Empathetic AI

To understand the ethical dimensions of empathetic AI, we must first define what we mean by "ethical boundaries." In the context of AI, ethics is concerned with the moral implications of designing systems that interact with human emotions. Emotional AI is not just about mimicking emotions—it's about replicating the nuances of human emotional responses in a way that respects individual dignity, privacy, and autonomy.

Example 1: Emotional Manipulation in Marketing

One of the most controversial applications of empathetic AI is in marketing. With its ability to analyze and understand emotional cues, AI has the potential to manipulate consumer behavior by tailoring ads based on a person's emotional state. Imagine an AI that detects frustration or indecision and then delivers highly personalized ads aimed at calming the user and influencing their purchasing decisions. While effective, this kind of emotional manipulation raises ethical concerns.

Pro Tip: Ethical guidelines should ensure that AI is not used to exploit vulnerabilities for commercial gain. Transparency is key, and businesses must be upfront about how their AI systems are processing emotional data.

Example 2: The AI Therapist Dilemma

AI systems are being introduced into sensitive fields like mental health, with chatbots designed to provide emotional support and guidance. These systems can analyze text or voice tone to understand a person's emotional state and offer advice or empathy. However, can an algorithm truly replicate the depth of understanding that a human therapist offers? Moreover, if an AI system gives inappropriate advice, who is responsible? These are complex ethical questions that need to be addressed as AI continues to play a role in mental health.

Pro Tip: It's crucial that AI in mental health be integrated with human oversight. While AI can supplement care, it should never replace human judgment, especially in sensitive areas like emotional and psychological well-being.

2. The Risk of Dehumanization

One of the most significant ethical concerns in the development of empathetic AI is the potential for dehumanization. If AI systems are designed to simulate empathy, could they replace genuine human interactions? The idea of forming emotional attachments to machines is troubling because, at its core, AI lacks the true emotional depth and understanding that humans offer one another.

Example 1: Virtual Companions for the Elderly

Robots like **Pepper** and other virtual companions are being deployed to offer companionship to the elderly, particularly in assisted living facilities. While these systems provide much-needed social interaction, there is a real concern that over-reliance on these machines could lead to further isolation. If robots are designed to be too empathetic, the elderly might choose to interact more with machines than with people.

Pro Tip: AI should never replace human relationships. Instead, it should serve as a complementary tool, encouraging individuals to connect with their families and communities.

Example 2: Emotional Dependency on AI Assistants

Imagine a world where people form deep emotional bonds with their AI assistants, such as **Siri** or **Alexa**. These systems can simulate empathy and respond to users in ways that foster a sense of connection. However, the more users rely on these systems for emotional support, the more they risk losing genuine human connections. This emotional dependency on machines could have far-reaching consequences on human relationships and mental health.

Pro Tip: Encourage healthy boundaries in human-AI interactions by designing systems that promote human connection rather than emotional reliance on machines. For example, AI systems could encourage users to engage with friends, family, or counselors for support rather than relying on the AI alone.

. . .

3. Manipulating Empathy: Ethical Concerns in Marketing and Advertising

As AI becomes more adept at understanding and replicating human emotions, it also opens the door for manipulation. Advertisers and marketers can use empathetic AI to design campaigns that appeal directly to consumers' emotional states. This raises serious ethical concerns, especially when companies use these technologies to exploit vulnerable individuals.

Example 1: Emotional Targeting in Retail

AI systems can analyze social media posts, browsing history, and even facial expressions to gauge a person's emotional state. Armed with this information, marketers can craft highly targeted ads designed to elicit specific emotional reactions. While this can make marketing more effective, it also opens the door to manipulation.

Pro Tip: AI in marketing should be used responsibly. Clear consent should be obtained from users before collecting emotional data, and AI should not be used to pressure or manipulate customers into making purchases.

Example 2: AI-Generated Content and Emotional Manipulation

Social media platforms increasingly use AI to curate content that resonates emotionally with users. By using algorithms to predict the types of content that will generate the most emotional engagement, platforms can boost user interaction but also risk creating echo chambers or spreading misinformation. This is particularly problematic when emotionally charged content is used to sway political opinions or promote divisive messages.

Pro Tip: AI systems used in content curation should be

transparent about how they select and promote content. Platforms must prioritize ethical guidelines that discourage the manipulation of emotions for political or financial gain.

4. Accountability and Transparency in Empathetic AI

As emotional AI systems become more prevalent, the issue of accountability is increasingly important. When an AI system causes harm—whether through misinterpretation of emotional cues, misuse of data, or manipulation—who is responsible? Should the developers, the company deploying the system, or the AI itself be held accountable? These questions are central to ensuring that empathetic AI is developed ethically.

Example 1: Misinterpretation of Emotional Cues

AI systems designed to interact emotionally with humans can sometimes misinterpret emotional signals, leading to inappropriate responses. For instance, an AI system might misread a user's frustration as happiness, leading to an inadequate or even harmful response.

Pro Tip: Developers must rigorously test AI systems to ensure that they accurately interpret emotional cues and provide responses that align with the user's true emotional state.

Example 2: Lack of Transparency in Data Usage

AI systems often rely on vast amounts of personal data to function effectively. However, many users are unaware of how their emotional data is being used or who has access to it. This lack of transparency can undermine trust in AI systems and fuel concerns about privacy.

Pro Tip: Developers and companies must provide clear, concise information about how emotional data is being collected, stored, and used. Users should have full control over their data, including the ability to opt out of data collection.

5. The Path Forward: Ethical AI in a Connected World

The future of empathetic AI depends on the establishment of ethical frameworks that govern its development and deployment. As AI becomes more integrated into daily life, it is critical that we build systems that enhance human connections, rather than erode them. These frameworks must prioritize transparency, fairness, and respect for human dignity.

Example 1: Developing Ethical Guidelines

Organizations like the **AI Ethics Initiative** and **IEEE** are working on frameworks that address the ethical challenges posed by AI, including the safe and responsible use of emotional AI.

Pro Tip: Stay informed about these ethical guidelines and ensure that your AI systems comply with them to foster trust and ensure that emotional AI is used responsibly.

Example 2: Human-AI Collaboration

Rather than replacing human interactions, empathetic AI should augment human relationships. For example, AI could be used to assist caregivers by providing emotional support to patients, while still leaving critical decisions to human caregivers.

Pro Tip: Design AI systems that complement human interactions. They should be tools that enhance emotional intelligence, not replace the need for human empathy and connection.

Example 3: Educating the Public on Ethical AI

Public awareness campaigns can play a key role in ensuring that people understand the ethical implications of

AI. This can empower users to make informed decisions about how they interact with AI systems and encourage developers to create transparent, responsible technologies.

Pro Tip: Advocate for public education on AI ethics. Promote dialogue around the potential risks and rewards of emotional AI to ensure that society as a whole is prepared for its impact.

CONCLUSION

As we venture further into the age of empathetic AI, the ethical considerations surrounding this technology will continue to evolve. While AI has the potential to improve human relationships and emotional well-being, it must be developed with a clear moral compass. By establishing ethical guidelines, ensuring transparency, and promoting human-AI collaboration, we can harness the power of emotional AI in a way that benefits society without crossing moral boundaries.

CHAPTER 7: LOVE IN THE TIME OF ALGORITHMS: HOW AI IS TRANSFORMING HUMAN RELATIONSHIPS AND INTIMACY

The intersection of love and technology has always been an area of fascination. From the earliest matchmaking services to the rise of dating apps, humans have long sought ways to find and enhance connections with others. In the digital age, however, the advent of AI is taking these connections to new and often unprecedented heights. With the rise of algorithms designed to predict compatibility, curate meaningful conversations, and even simulate emotional support, we must ask: How is AI transforming our understanding of love, intimacy, and human connection?

In this chapter, we will explore the ways AI is reshaping human relationships, from the way we meet and form romantic connections to the ways technology is influencing our emotional bonds. We will also address the complexities and challenges posed by these advances, particularly the ethical implications of relying on AI in intimate contexts.

1. AI in Online Dating: Redefining Compatibility

Online dating platforms have long used algorithms to match users based on basic criteria such as location, interests, and preferences. However, AI is now taking matchmaking to a deeper, more nuanced level. By analyzing vast amounts of data—including personality traits, past relationship patterns, and even social media interactions—AI systems are better able to predict long-term compatibility than ever before.

Example 1: Tinder's Smart Matching Algorithm

Tinder, one of the world's most popular dating apps, uses AI-powered algorithms to create "smart" matches between users. The app takes into account factors like past swiping behavior, mutual interests, and even how long a person spends looking at a profile before swiping left or right. Over time, Tinder's algorithm "learns" users' preferences and fine-tunes match suggestions, attempting to improve compatibility predictions.

Pro Tip: When using dating apps, keep in mind that AI is only one part of the equation. While algorithms may improve matchmaking, the human element—communication, shared experiences, and emotional compatibility—remains essential to a successful relationship.

2. AI-Assisted Conversations: The Evolution of Communication

AI-powered chatbots and virtual assistants are being used to facilitate conversations between individuals, acting as intermediaries that help break the ice, suggest topics for discussion, and even provide emotional support. But can these AI tools truly foster meaningful conversations, or are they merely offering a shallow substitute for authentic human interaction?

Example 1: Replika – A Virtual Companion for Emotional Support

Replika is an AI chatbot designed to act as a virtual companion, offering users a space to express their feelings, thoughts, and emotions. The bot learns from each interaction, attempting to adapt to the user's emotional needs over time. Although Replika cannot fully replicate the emotional depth of human relationships, many users find comfort in its conversations, especially in times of loneliness or stress.

Pro Tip: While AI companions can provide temporary relief from loneliness, they cannot replace the complex emotional intimacy that comes with human relationships. Use AI as a supplement, not a substitute, for meaningful social connections.

Example 2: AI-Enhanced Dating Profiles

Some dating apps are integrating AI to help users craft more compelling profiles by analyzing successful patterns from other profiles and suggesting changes to improve match rates. These AI systems can even suggest specific phrases or conversation starters that might increase the likelihood of a response.

Pro Tip: Use AI-generated suggestions to enhance your profile, but ensure that your personality shines through. Genuine connections are formed when authenticity is prioritized over algorithmic optimization.

3. AI and Emotional Support: Navigating the Boundaries of Intimacy

AI is being used in therapy and mental health to offer emotional support, but as the technology grows more advanced, the line between human and machine emotions becomes increasingly blurred. While some might appreciate the convenience and privacy of AI-based emotional support, others are concerned about the emotional risks of forming attachments to machines.

Example 1: AI Therapy Bots like Woebot

Woebot is an AI-driven chatbot designed to offer mental health support using cognitive-behavioral therapy (CBT) techniques. It's been shown to help users manage stress, anxiety, and other mental health challenges. While Woebot provides immediate, accessible support, it raises questions about whether AI can effectively replace human therapists or merely serve as a temporary solution.

Pro Tip: AI mental health tools can provide helpful strategies and coping mechanisms, but they should be used alongside professional therapy if you're dealing with serious emotional or psychological issues. Always seek human expertise when needed.

4. The Challenges of Love and AI: Ethical Implications

As AI begins to play a larger role in our intimate lives, new ethical dilemmas arise. Should we allow AI to simulate love and emotional intimacy? How does our dependence on technology affect our capacity for real human relationships? In this section, we'll delve into the ethical challenges and explore potential solutions to ensure that AI serves humanity in healthy ways.

Example 1: AI and Consent in Relationship Technologies

With the increasing use of AI in relationships, it's crucial to address issues of consent. Dating apps, chatbots, and virtual assistants often collect and process sensitive emotional data, and users need to be aware of the extent to which this data is being used. Should AI systems be required to ask for explicit consent before gathering data or providing emotional responses?

Pro Tip: Transparency is essential when it comes to AI in relationships. Users should be clearly informed about what data is being collected and how it will be used. Consent should be an ongoing, rather than one-time, process.

5. The Future of Love and AI: What's Next?

The future of AI and human relationships is full of potential, but it also holds many uncertainties. As AI systems become more adept at simulating emotions, there is the potential for a radical shift in how we view love and intimacy. Will we one day form genuine emotional connections with machines, or will the human heart always crave the complexity and unpredictability of real relationships?

Example 1: The Rise of AI-Generated Romance Novels

Some AI systems are already being used to write romance novels, generating plots that cater to the emotional and romantic needs of readers. These AI-generated stories tap into human desires and fantasies, but they raise the question of whether AI can truly understand love in the way humans do.

Pro Tip: As AI-generated content becomes more pervasive, it's important to remember that these stories are simulations based on patterns and algorithms. Real-life love and relationships are far more complex, messy, and unique than any machine could predict.

CONCLUSION: Embracing the Evolution of Love

While AI has the potential to transform the way we

experience love, intimacy, and relationships, it's important to approach these developments with care and consideration. AI tools can help us navigate the complexities of modern romance, but they should never replace the emotional depth that comes with genuine human connection. As we continue to integrate AI into our personal lives, we must strike a balance between technological convenience and the richness of human emotion, ensuring that our relationships—whether human or machine—remain rooted in trust, authenticity, and empathy.

Pro Tip: Use AI to enhance your emotional intelligence and improve your relationships, but always prioritize real, face-to-face connections. No algorithm can replace the beauty of genuine human interaction.

CHAPTER 8: EMPATHY IN BUSINESS: AI AND CUSTOMER EXPERIENCE

I n today's competitive business landscape, customers have higher expectations than ever before. They don't just want quality products or services; they want to feel understood, valued, and emotionally connected to the brands they interact with. This has led many companies to explore how Artificial Intelligence (AI) can help enhance customer experiences, particularly through emotional AI, which aims to replicate human empathy. But what does this look like in practice? How can businesses use AI to foster deeper, more meaningful engagement with their customers?

In this chapter, we'll explore the exciting world of emotional AI and how it is being used to improve customer service, create personalized experiences, and enhance brand loyalty. Through several real-world examples, we'll see how AI is reshaping the customer experience, allowing businesses to anticipate needs, understand emotions, and respond in ways that feel authentically human.

. . .

1. AI in Customer Service: The Rise of Empathetic Chatbots

For years, businesses have been using chatbots to handle customer service inquiries. But while these bots were originally designed to automate basic tasks, new AI advancements have enabled them to exhibit more emotional intelligence, improving interactions with customers.

Example 1: Ada's AI-Powered Customer Service Chatbot

Ada is an AI chatbot that uses machine learning to recognize customer emotions based on the tone, language, and context of their inquiries. This allows Ada to respond more empathetically, offering personalized solutions and guiding customers through their problems in a manner that feels attentive and caring.

Pro Tip: For AI-powered customer service systems, focus on training your bots to recognize emotions through text and speech analysis. This helps them respond with empathy and improves the overall customer experience.

2. Personalization at Scale: Understanding Customer Preferences

One of the most powerful aspects of emotional AI is its ability to personalize customer interactions on a massive scale. By analyzing customer data—such as past purchases, browsing habits, and social media activity—AI can predict what a customer might need or want before they even ask.

Example 1: Netflix's Personalized Recommendations

Netflix uses AI to analyze viewing history and preferences, creating personalized recommendations that cater to individual tastes. The platform's algorithms can detect what genres, actors, and themes a viewer is drawn to, offering suggestions that feel tailored to their unique emotional preferences.

Pro Tip: To maximize AI-driven personalization, leverage customer data responsibly. Ensure that your AI systems are continuously learning from past interactions, and remember that customers value privacy. Be transparent about what data you're collecting and why.

3. Voice Assistants and Emotional Tone: Humanizing Technology

Voice assistants like Amazon's Alexa, Google Assistant, and Apple's Siri are no longer just basic tools for setting timers or checking the weather. With emotional AI, these voice assistants are becoming more attuned to the tone of the user's voice, helping them respond with more appropriate emotional intelligence.

Example 1: Google Assistant's Emotional Sensitivity

Google Assistant has made strides in improving its emotional intelligence. By analyzing the emotional tone of a user's voice, it can adjust its responses to be more empathetic. For example, if a user expresses frustration or sadness, Google Assistant can soften its tone and offer more thoughtful responses, making the interaction feel less transactional and more human.

Pro Tip: Implement AI voice recognition technology that can detect emotional cues from users' tones and alter the assistant's responses accordingly. This helps foster more authentic and human-like customer experiences.

4. Empathy in Marketing: Connecting Through Emotion

Marketing strategies are no longer just about selling

products—they are about creating emotional connections with customers. By using AI to analyze customer sentiment, businesses can craft more emotionally resonant marketing campaigns that speak directly to the customer's needs, desires, and values.

Example 1: Coca-Cola's Emotional AI in Advertising

Coca-Cola has experimented with emotional AI to gauge the sentiment of its advertisements and ensure they resonate with viewers. By using AI to track social media reactions and customer feedback, Coca-Cola can refine its messaging and create ads that evoke positive emotional responses.

Pro Tip: Use AI to analyze the sentiment of your marketing campaigns and adjust them in real-time. Emotional AI can help you create messaging that connects with customers on a deeper emotional level, leading to stronger brand loyalty.

5. Ethical Considerations: Striking the Right Balance

As businesses incorporate more AI into their customer experiences, it's crucial to address the ethical implications of using emotional intelligence in AI. While AI can enhance customer service, personalization, and marketing, it also raises questions about privacy, trust, and manipulation.

Example 1: AI Ethics in Customer Data

Brands like Apple and Microsoft have taken steps to address ethical concerns around the collection and use of customer data. By being transparent about their data practices and giving customers control over their information, these companies are fostering trust and creating more ethical AI systems.

Pro Tip: Always be transparent with customers about

the data you collect and how it is used. Use AI ethically to enhance customer experiences, but ensure that privacy and trust remain top priorities.

Conclusion: **The Future of Empathy in Business**

The potential for AI to enhance customer experiences through empathy is vast, but it requires careful attention to ethical considerations and emotional intelligence. As businesses continue to leverage emotional AI, they must be mindful of the fine line between creating deeper connections and crossing into manipulation.

By using AI to recognize emotions, personalize experiences, and provide empathetic interactions, businesses can create meaningful relationships with their customers. The future of AI in business is one where technology and humanity coexist in a way that fosters trust, loyalty, and authentic connections.

Pro Tip: As AI continues to evolve, stay ahead of the curve by experimenting with new emotional intelligence technologies. Embrace AI as a tool for empathy, not just efficiency, and always prioritize the human element in your customer relationships.

CHAPTER 9: CULTURAL BIASES IN EMPATHY MACHINES: EXAMINING DIVERSITY AND BIAS IN EMOTIONAL ALGORITHMS

As artificial intelligence (AI) systems become increasingly integrated into our daily lives, one of the most pressing issues to address is the potential for bias within these technologies. Emotional AI, designed to recognize and respond to human emotions, is no exception. While these systems have the potential to improve customer experiences, mental health support, and even interpersonal relationships, they also risk perpetuating and amplifying societal biases that exist in the data they are trained on. In this chapter, we will explore the challenges and ethical considerations of cultural bias in emotional AI systems, discuss how these biases arise, and look at what steps can be taken to create more inclusive and equitable AI technologies.

1. Understanding Cultural Bias in AI

AI systems, including emotional AI, are trained on vast amounts of data—often sourced from human interactions, social media, and other public forums. The problem arises when these data sets reflect societal biases—whether racial, gender-based, socio-economic, or cultural—that are inherent in the source material. These biases can then be coded into the algorithms themselves, resulting in AI systems that might interpret emotions, behaviors, or responses inaccurately or unfairly based on the user's background.

Example 1: Gender and Racial Bias in Voice Recognition

Several studies have shown that voice recognition systems, including those used in emotional AI, often exhibit bias towards certain accents, genders, and ethnicities. For instance, a 2019 study revealed that AI voice assistants like Amazon's Alexa and Apple's Siri performed less accurately for African American Vernacular English (AAVE) speakers compared to standard American English speakers. These biases can result in misinterpretation of emotions or miscommunication, which can undermine the empathy that these systems are meant to provide.

Pro Tip: To mitigate gender and racial bias, AI systems should be trained on diverse datasets that accurately reflect the range of accents, dialects, and cultural nuances that users may present. Regular audits and adjustments of AI training data are crucial to ensure more accurate and empathetic interactions.

2. How Emotional AI Misreads Cultural Norms

Cultural differences heavily influence how emotions are expressed and perceived. What may be considered a sign of respect, politeness, or sincerity in one culture may be perceived as disinterest or even rudeness in another. Emotional AI systems, however, are often designed based on

Western models of emotional expression, which can lead to significant misunderstandings when these systems interact with users from different cultural backgrounds.

Example 1: Misinterpretation of Non-Western Emotions

In some Asian cultures, for example, indirect communication is often preferred, and people may suppress their emotional responses to avoid confrontation or maintain harmony. An AI system trained on more direct or expressive emotional norms might misinterpret a user's tone or response, wrongly assuming that the person is upset or disengaged.

Pro Tip: Emotional AI systems must be trained on culturally diverse emotional expressions and behavioral norms to better understand and respond to users from various backgrounds. This will help create AI that is more universally empathetic and able to adapt to different cultural contexts.

3. Impact of Bias on User Trust and Relationship Building

The presence of cultural bias in AI can erode trust between users and AI systems. If a user feels that an AI is misjudging their emotional state based on inaccurate cultural assumptions, they may be less likely to engage with the system in the future. Trust is a crucial element in the effectiveness of empathy machines, and when trust is compromised, the AI's ability to connect with users in meaningful ways diminishes.

Example 1: The Backlash Against Biased AI Systems

In 2018, Amazon scrapped its AI recruitment tool after discovering that it was biased against women. The system, which was designed to help identify top candidates for technical roles, was trained on resumes that were predominantly male. As a result, the AI favored resumes from male candidates, reinforcing the gender bias in the hiring process. This example highlights how biased AI can damage relationships between businesses and their customers or users.

Pro Tip: To build trust with users, businesses should ensure that their AI systems are both inclusive and transparent about how they are trained. Being upfront about efforts to combat bias and implementing feedback loops where users can report inaccuracies will foster greater user confidence.

4. Ethical Implications: The Role of Developers in Preventing Bias

AI developers have a responsibility to address bias in their systems proactively. Emotional AI is designed to replicate empathy, but if it reflects the biases present in society, it can unintentionally perpetuate inequalities. Developers must prioritize inclusivity by ensuring that diverse perspectives are involved in the creation, testing, and refinement of AI systems.

Example 1: IBM's Commitment to Ethical AI Development

IBM has made significant strides in promoting ethical AI, setting up a framework that addresses biases in AI systems and emphasizes transparency. In 2019, IBM introduced tools to help businesses detect and mitigate bias in their AI models. By providing these tools to companies, IBM has set an example for others in the industry to follow, highlighting the importance of making AI systems fairer and more inclusive.

Pro Tip: Developers should work with interdisciplinary

teams that include individuals from different cultural, racial, and gender backgrounds to ensure AI systems are trained with diverse perspectives. Regularly updating AI models and testing them in varied real-world scenarios will help identify potential biases.

5. Addressing Cultural Bias in Empathy Machines: The Path Forward

The future of emotional AI lies in its ability to understand and respond to the diversity of human experience. As AI continues to play a larger role in our daily interactions, it is essential that the technology evolves to be more inclusive and culturally sensitive. While there is still much work to be done, significant strides are being made to create emotional AI systems that are both effective and equitable.

Example 1: Google's AI for Cultural Sensitivity

Google's AI research team has focused on enhancing the cultural sensitivity of its virtual assistants by designing them to better recognize and understand diverse linguistic and emotional cues. This includes updating voice assistants to acknowledge regional accents and dialects, as well as cultural differences in emotional expression.

Pro Tip: Companies should actively seek input from cultural experts, psychologists, and sociologists to help shape the design and development of emotional AI systems. Collaborating with local communities to understand the cultural nuances of emotional expression can significantly improve the effectiveness of empathy machines.

CONCLUSION: Building Empathetic, Unbiased AI Systems

Emotional AI holds incredible potential to revolutionize

how we interact with technology, from providing personalized customer service to offering mental health support. However, for these systems to be truly effective, they must be free from bias—particularly cultural bias—that may limit their ability to connect with people from diverse backgrounds. By actively addressing these issues and fostering inclusivity in AI development, we can ensure that emotional AI lives up to its promise of empathy, understanding, and human connection for all.

Pro Tip: Continual education, collaboration, and transparency in AI development will be key to mitigating bias. As AI technology advances, it is essential to ensure that it works for everyone, respecting cultural differences and promoting deeper, more meaningful engagement with users.

CHAPTER 10: THE CREATIVITY CONUNDRUM: EMOTIONAL AI IN MUSIC, ART, AND STORYTELLING

The rise of Artificial Intelligence (AI) has not only impacted industries like business and healthcare but has also made its mark in the world of creativity. From music and art to storytelling and design, AI systems are being used to generate new and innovative forms of human expression. But when machines create, can they truly be considered creative? And what does it mean for human creativity if emotional AI can replicate or even enhance the artistic process?

In this chapter, we will delve into the complex relationship between emotional AI and creativity, exploring how AI is reshaping the fields of music, art, and storytelling. Through a series of fascinating examples, we'll examine the potential of AI to produce work that resonates emotionally with audiences, while also questioning whether machines can ever truly replicate the depth of human creativity.

1. AI in Music: Composing Emotional Soundscapes

Music has long been considered one of the most emotionally expressive forms of art. The ability to evoke feelings—joy, sadness, nostalgia, or excitement—through melody, harmony, and rhythm has made music a universal language. But can an AI understand and create music that connects with listeners on an emotional level? With advancements in AI-driven music composition, the answer is becoming clearer.

Example 1: OpenAI's MuseNet

OpenAI's MuseNet is a powerful example of AI's ability to compose music. Trained on a vast dataset of compositions across genres, MuseNet can generate original pieces in the style of various musicians—from Beethoven to The Beatles. What's particularly impressive is that MuseNet doesn't just replicate existing songs; it creates entirely new compositions that blend styles and evoke emotions.

Pro Tip: Emotional AI in music composition can be enhanced by teaching the system to recognize emotional cues within different genres. For instance, classical music might be associated with feelings of calm or nostalgia, while pop music can evoke excitement or joy.

2. AI in Art: From Pixels to Paintings

Much like music, visual art relies on the artist's ability to express deep emotions, thoughts, and perspectives through color, form, and composition. As AI tools become more advanced, they are beginning to create artwork that evokes similar emotions and responses to that of human-created art.

Example 1: The Portrait of Edmond de Belamy

One of the most notable examples of AI-generated art is

"Portrait of Edmond de Belamy," a painting created by the Paris-based art collective Obvious using a machine learning algorithm called GAN (Generative Adversarial Network). The piece sold at auction for over $432,000, sparking a conversation about the value of AI art. The painting portrays a historical figure but with ghostly, almost other-worldly features—an effect that arose from the AI's attempt to generate an image that mimics the aesthetic of classical portraiture.

Pro Tip: Emotional AI can be used to analyze color psychology and composition theory, helping machines understand the emotional impact of different visual elements. This way, AI-generated art can align more closely with human emotional responses.

3. AI in Storytelling: Crafting Narratives with Emotion

Storytelling is at the heart of human experience, whether through literature, film, or oral traditions. Stories have the power to inspire, connect, and even heal. But can an AI create a story that resonates with human emotions, capturing the subtleties of narrative structure and character development? AI is now beginning to venture into this territory, with some remarkable results.

Example 1: AI Writing Short Stories with Deep Emotional Impact

In 2016, the AI platform "Benjamin," developed by the creative studio Botnik, was used to generate short stories that mimic the writing styles of famous authors like J.K. Rowling and George Orwell. While some of the stories were comedic, others evoked genuine emotional responses from readers. This sparked a broader conversation about the potential for AI to write stories that not only entertain but also elicit complex emotions.

Pro Tip: To improve emotional AI in storytelling, focus on teaching machines narrative arcs, character development, and emotional pacing. Algorithms that can mimic the emotional highs and lows of a traditional story can lead to richer, more engaging narratives.

4. The Ethical Implications of AI in Creative Arts

As AI becomes more involved in creative processes, a crucial question arises: who owns the rights to AI-generated art? Is the artist the creator of the algorithm, or does the machine itself hold some claim to the work? Additionally, how do we ensure that AI does not inadvertently copy or plagiarize existing works while generating its own?

Example 1: The Copyright Debate in AI-Generated Art

In 2018, a U.S. court ruled that works created solely by AI cannot be copyrighted. This has sparked debate about the legal status of AI-generated works and whether the humans who program these systems should be credited as the creators. This issue has profound implications for how we view creativity and ownership in the digital age.

Pro Tip: When integrating AI into the creative process, it's important for creators and technologists to consider the ethical implications, including issues of authorship, originality, and intellectual property.

5. The Future of AI and Creativity: Collaboration or Competition?

While AI has shown remarkable abilities in generating

music, art, and stories, it remains to be seen whether it can ever fully replicate the depth of human creativity. Some argue that AI is simply a tool—a powerful assistant for human artists—but others believe that AI could one-day rival human creativity, blurring the lines between machine and human-made art. So, what does the future hold for AI and creativity?

Example 1: AI-Assisted Artistic Collaboration

Rather than seeing AI as a competitor, many artists are beginning to see it as a collaborator. AI systems like Deep-Dream, developed by Google, allow artists to generate unique visual effects and designs that would be difficult or impossible to create manually. These collaborative efforts between humans and machines are pushing the boundaries of art and creativity.

Pro Tip: Embrace AI as a collaborative tool rather than as a replacement for human creativity. By combining the unique strengths of AI—its ability to generate vast amounts of data and analyze patterns—with human intuition and emotion, we can create truly groundbreaking artistic works.

CONCLUSION: **Creativity in the Age of Emotional AI**

Emotional AI is rapidly changing the way we think about creativity. Whether it's composing music, creating visual art, or crafting stories, AI has demonstrated the potential to produce emotionally resonant works that rival human-created content. However, while AI may be able to mimic aspects of human creativity, it still lacks the true depth of human experience and emotion that fuels most artistic expression.

Pro Tip: As AI continues to evolve, creators must view

emotional AI as a tool for enhancing and augmenting their creative processes, rather than replacing the human touch. By using AI to explore new possibilities in music, art, and storytelling, we can push the boundaries of what's possible and discover new forms of artistic expression that blend the best of both human and machine creativity.

CHAPTER 11: CHILDREN AND EMPATHETIC TECH: AI'S INFLUENCE ON YOUNG MINDS

As Artificial Intelligence (AI) becomes increasingly woven into the fabric of our daily lives, its impact on children has drawn both excitement and concern. From virtual assistants and educational tools to AI-powered toys and digital therapists, children are interacting with AI systems at younger ages than ever before. In this chapter, we will explore how empathetic AI is shaping young minds, influencing their emotional development, social interactions, and the ways they perceive the world. We'll also examine the ethical implications and the potential risks of allowing AI into children's lives.

1. Emotional AI and Child Development

The human brain is remarkably adaptable during early childhood, absorbing social, emotional, and cognitive cues to develop a sense of self, empathy, and connection. In this sensitive developmental stage, AI can have both positive and negative effects on children's emotional growth.

Example 1: AI-Powered Educational Assistants

AI-driven educational tools like the "CAMPiN" AI assistant, designed to teach empathy, can help children with autism spectrum disorder (ASD) understand emotions better. These tools use facial recognition and interactive dialogue to guide children in recognizing facial expressions, body language, and tone of voice. By responding to these emotional cues, children can learn appropriate social behaviors and emotional responses.

Pro Tip: AI-powered educational tools should be designed with developmental psychology principles in mind. They must adapt to the child's learning pace and provide positive reinforcement to encourage emotional growth, rather than simply instructing them on what to do.

2. AI in Virtual Companions and Emotional Support

Children who grow up interacting with AI-powered virtual companions are forming relationships with machines at a foundational level. These virtual companions, designed to provide companionship, support, and even empathy, are often presented as characters that children can talk to, confide in, and develop bonds with.

Example 1: The Role of AI in Mental Health for Children

AI-based apps like Woebot have been developed to provide mental health support for both children and adults. Woebot is a chatbot that offers cognitive behavioral therapy (CBT) techniques to help children deal with stress, anxiety, and other emotional challenges. By using AI, these systems can detect patterns in a child's speech or behavior to offer relevant coping strategies and advice.

Pro Tip: It's important that AI companions for children be equipped with safeguards to ensure their interactions remain healthy and appropriate. These systems must avoid over-reliance on AI for emotional support, encouraging children to seek real-world help when needed.

3. The Role of AI in Shaping Empathy and Social Skills

Empathy is one of the most important emotional skills children develop, and AI's role in this process is becoming increasingly significant. By interacting with empathetic machines, children may develop a more nuanced understanding of how to connect with others on an emotional level.

Example 1: AI's Impact on Social Skills in Children

Research has shown that children who engage with AI programs that encourage emotional recognition and social interaction show improved social skills. For example, interactive robots like "KIBO," which is used in classrooms, teach children how to communicate emotions and solve problems collaboratively. These tools help children build emotional intelligence (EQ), an essential skill for success in life.

Pro Tip: The key to developing children's empathy through AI lies in designing systems that not only respond to emotions but also teach children how to express their own feelings appropriately. As children grow, they can use these early lessons to build healthier, more empathetic relationships with others.

4. Risks of Overreliance on AI for Emotional Development

While AI systems can provide emotional learning opportunities, there are also significant risks associated with too much reliance on these machines, particularly for young children. Overuse of AI for emotional or social interactions can hinder children's ability to develop genuine human relationships and their understanding of real-world social cues.

Example 1: The Problem of Social Isolation

Research suggests that children who engage more with AI-powered toys or virtual assistants can experience social isolation. These children might become overly attached to their AI companions and have difficulty building real-world friendships or understanding complex human emotions. Moreover, children might struggle to differentiate between real emotional connections and programmed responses.

Pro Tip: It's essential to strike a balance between AI interaction and real-world socialization. While AI can be a helpful tool for learning, children should be encouraged to engage with human peers, family members, and adults to ensure healthy emotional and social development.

5. Ethical Considerations: Should We Be Programming Empathy into Machines for Children?

The idea of programming empathy into machines that interact with children raises serious ethical concerns. What are the implications of children forming emotional bonds with AI systems? Is it ethical to create machines that seem capable of understanding or even fostering emotional responses, especially when these machines may not be able to understand the complexities of human emotions?

Example 1: The Ethical Debate Surrounding AI and Child Development

In 2017, an ethical debate was sparked when the toy company Mattel released "Hello Barbie," a doll powered by AI that could carry on conversations with children. The doll was marketed as an empathetic friend that children could confide in. However, critics raised concerns about privacy, data collection, and the potential for emotional manipulation. The toy's ability to respond emotionally to children's thoughts and questions seemed to blur the line between real human empathy and a machine-generated response.

Pro Tip: To address the ethical dilemmas posed by AI in children's lives, developers should adhere to strict privacy guidelines, transparency, and parental controls. Furthermore, AI systems must be transparent about their limitations, ensuring that children understand they are interacting with machines and not real people.

CONCLUSION: Navigating the Future of AI and Children's Emotional Development

As AI continues to evolve and become more integrated into children's lives, it's essential for parents, educators, and developers to carefully consider its impact on emotional growth and development. While AI has the potential to support children in understanding their emotions, building social skills, and enhancing empathy, there are also significant challenges to ensure that these technologies are used ethically and appropriately.

Pro Tip: Encouraging healthy, balanced interactions between children and empathetic AI can help them develop emotional intelligence and empathy while maintaining strong human relationships. With careful attention to ethical concerns, transparency, and real-world connections, we can ensure that AI benefits children's emotional development rather than hinders it.

The future of children and AI holds great promise, but it is up to all of us to guide this powerful technology with care, ensuring it supports and enhances the development of future generations.

CHAPTER 12: THE FUTURE OF WORK AND EMOTIONAL AI: HOW AI RESHAPES EMPATHY IN PROFESSIONAL ENVIRONMENTS

As we move further into the digital age, one of the most significant shifts in the workplace is the increasing integration of Artificial Intelligence (AI) into the very fabric of professional interactions. AI is no longer confined to just automating tasks or analyzing data; it is beginning to play a crucial role in shaping how we interact with each other in the workplace. Emotional AI—systems capable of detecting, responding to, and replicating emotional responses—has emerged as a game-changer in transforming the way empathy is expressed in professional environments.

In this chapter, we will explore how AI is reshaping empathy in the workplace, providing both opportunities and challenges for organizations, employees, and leaders. From enhancing customer service to improving internal communication, emotional AI is influencing how people collaborate, negotiate, and connect within their professional roles.

. . .

1. AI and the Evolution of Workplace Communication

Communication is at the heart of every business, and with emotional AI, it is becoming more nuanced. AI tools are being developed to detect emotional cues, not just from words, but from tone, body language, and facial expressions. In a virtual or hybrid work environment, where face-to-face interaction is limited, this can be an invaluable asset for maintaining healthy, empathetic communication.

Example 1: Virtual Communication Assistants

With the rise of remote work, many companies are adopting virtual assistants like Zoom's integrated AI that can monitor participant's emotional states through facial recognition technology. These tools can help managers gauge how employees feel during meetings, identifying disengagement or discomfort, and allowing them to adjust their approach accordingly. For instance, if a team member shows signs of frustration, the AI may suggest a more supportive communication strategy to the manager.

Pro Tip: When using emotional AI for workplace communication, it's vital to ensure that employees are informed and comfortable with the data being gathered. Transparency about how AI is being used can foster trust and encourage its positive impact on interactions.

2. Empathy in Customer Service: Enhancing User Experience with Emotional AI

Customer service has been one of the key areas where emotional AI has found rapid application. AI systems, from chatbots to voice assistants, are now being equipped with the ability to detect customer emotions and respond empathetically. This allows businesses to build stronger customer relationships, resolve issues more efficiently, and ensure a more personalized service.

Example 1: IBM Watson in Customer Support

IBM Watson has integrated emotional intelligence into its customer service solutions. Watson can analyze customer interactions, such as phone calls or live chats, and assess the emotional tone of a customer's language. Based on this analysis, Watson can provide tailored responses that show empathy and understanding, improving overall customer satisfaction.

Pro Tip: Companies should ensure that emotional AI in customer service doesn't replace human empathy but rather augments it. For more complex issues or deeply emotional situations, human agents should be ready to step in to provide the necessary support.

3. Emotional AI for Employee Well-Being and Mental Health

As mental health awareness in the workplace rises, companies are increasingly turning to AI to support employee well-being. Emotional AI can help detect signs of burnout, stress, or emotional fatigue, offering real-time solutions or recommendations for intervention. These tools can serve as an early warning system, allowing companies to address mental health issues before they escalate.

Example 1: Well-Being Programs with AI

One leading example is the AI-driven platform *Headspace for Work*, which offers mental health support for employees by combining mindfulness techniques with emotional AI. The system tracks mood and behavior patterns over time, offering personalized mindfulness exercises or tips for stress management. This data helps HR teams monitor overall employee well-being, leading to a more proactive approach to workplace mental health.

Pro Tip: While emotional AI in mental health applications can be helpful, it should never replace professional mental health services. Companies should use AI to complement, not substitute, traditional mental health support systems, providing employees with the resources they need to thrive.

4. Bias and Fairness: Avoiding the Pitfalls of Emotional AI

One of the biggest challenges with emotional AI in the workplace is ensuring fairness and avoiding bias. AI systems are only as good as the data they are trained on, and if these data sets are flawed or incomplete, the system can inadvertently perpetuate biases in decision-making, communication, or employee evaluations. For instance, AI systems that are trained predominantly on data from a single demographic may not interpret emotional cues accurately when interacting with employees or customers from diverse backgrounds.

Example 1: Bias in Performance Evaluations

An AI tool designed to evaluate employee performance based on emotional responses during meetings or presentations could unintentionally show bias if it's trained only on data from a homogenous group of employees. For example, the AI might misinterpret the tone or body language of employees from different cultural backgrounds, leading to biased performance reviews.

Pro Tip: To mitigate bias, emotional AI systems should be trained on diverse datasets that represent the wide range of human experiences, ensuring fair and accurate emotional recognition across all employees and customers.

. . .

5. The Future of Leadership: AI as a Tool for Empathetic Leadership

Leadership is inherently tied to emotional intelligence. Effective leaders not only direct teams but also build trust, inspire, and motivate through empathy. With the rise of emotional AI, there is an opportunity for leaders to leverage these tools to enhance their own emotional intelligence, make better decisions, and understand their team's needs on a deeper level.

Example 1: AI-Driven Leadership Tools

AI systems, such as *Pymetrics*, are being used in leadership development programs to assess a leader's emotional intelligence and provide insights into how they can improve their approach to managing teams. These tools evaluate facial expressions, tone of voice, and other emotional signals to assess how leaders are perceived and how they can become more empathetic in their interactions.

Pro Tip: Emotional AI should not replace the human touch in leadership but serve as a supplement to enhance decision-making. By providing leaders with emotional insights, AI can enable them to take more informed, empathetic actions that strengthen relationships within the workplace.

6. The Role of Emotional AI in Recruitment and Talent Management

In the world of recruitment, emotional AI is transforming how companies assess candidates. Traditional recruitment methods focus on skills, experience, and education, but emotional AI is now being used to evaluate candidates' emotional intelligence, personality traits, and even cultural fit.

Example 1: AI-Powered Hiring Platforms

AI-powered platforms like *HireVue* are leveraging emotional AI to analyze candidates' facial expressions, tone of voice, and body language during video interviews. This analysis helps employers assess a candidate's emotional responses to certain questions, providing a more comprehensive view of their emotional intelligence and interpersonal skills.

Pro Tip: While emotional AI can be a useful tool in recruitment, it's crucial to combine it with traditional human judgment. Machines may be able to assess emotions, but they can't replace the nuanced understanding a human recruiter brings to the table.

CONCLUSION: **Navigating the Future of Work with Emotional AI**

The integration of emotional AI into the workplace is undeniably changing how we connect, communicate, and collaborate. Whether it's improving employee well-being, enhancing customer experiences, or supporting leadership development, emotional AI has the potential to redefine workplace dynamics. However, like any new technology, its success depends on how thoughtfully and ethically it is implemented.

Pro Tip: The future of work with emotional AI will be successful if companies prioritize transparency, ethical use, and a balance between technology and human interaction. By leveraging emotional AI as a tool to enhance, rather than replace, human connection, businesses can create a more empathetic, productive, and engaged workforce.

As emotional AI continues to evolve, it's important for leaders and organizations to stay ahead of the curve, embracing these technologies while ensuring they complement human empathy, rather than undermining it. The future of work will undoubtedly be shaped by AI, but the heart of any successful organization will always be its people.

CHAPTER 13: CRISIS RESPONSE WITH AI: EMPATHY-DRIVEN AI DURING DISASTERS AND EMERGENCIES

In times of crisis, whether it's a natural disaster, a global pandemic, or a humanitarian emergency, the ability to respond quickly and effectively can mean the difference between life and death. As we face increasingly complex global challenges, there is a growing recognition of the potential for Artificial Intelligence (AI) to aid in these critical situations. Beyond mere problem-solving, AI is being developed with an emphasis on empathy to help respond to crises in a way that not only saves lives but also supports the emotional well-being of those affected.

In this chapter, we will explore how AI—powered by emotional intelligence—is being deployed in disaster response efforts. From providing emotional support to victims to coordinating resource allocation and recovery efforts, AI's empathetic capabilities are becoming indispensable tools in the modern crisis management toolbox.

1. Emotional AI and Immediate Crisis Response

During an emergency, swift communication and

emotional support are essential. AI systems equipped with empathy-driven algorithms can step in to fill critical gaps where human resources are limited. These systems offer real-time emotional assistance, guiding affected individuals through trauma and anxiety, while providing critical information about the situation at hand.

Example 1: AI Chatbots in Crisis Communication

During the COVID-19 pandemic, many governments and organizations turned to AI chatbots to disseminate information and answer questions from people under quarantine or lockdown. For instance, the *WHO Health Alert* powered by WhatsApp was an AI-driven tool that provided real-time, accurate information about the pandemic, including how to prevent infection and how to access medical services. These bots were designed with empathetic responses to help calm fears and encourage preventative health measures.

Pro Tip: During crises, it's important that AI responses are sensitive to the emotional state of the individual. Using empathetic language—acknowledging fears, confusion, or frustration—can make a significant difference in how the message is received.

2. AI in Emergency Relief Coordination

AI-driven systems are playing an increasingly vital role in logistics, helping coordinate emergency relief efforts during natural disasters like earthquakes, hurricanes, and floods. These systems can analyze vast amounts of data—such as weather patterns, infrastructure damage, and population density—to predict the most effective ways to deliver aid and resources.

Example 1: AI in Earthquake Response

After the 2015 earthquake in Nepal, organizations like the *Red Cross* utilized AI algorithms to analyze satellite images and social media posts to pinpoint the areas most affected by the disaster. This allowed them to direct resources to places that needed them the most, enhancing the speed and precision of their response. AI also helped track the movements of people who may be trapped or displaced, ensuring that relief efforts were more efficient.

Pro Tip: In future disaster responses, AI tools should continue to be integrated into systems for logistics and resource allocation. Ensuring these tools are fully adaptable to different disaster types will maximize their potential and help save lives more effectively.

3. Emotional Support Through AI-Driven Mental Health Programs

Disasters take a heavy emotional toll, and mental health support is just as crucial as physical aid. In many instances, psychological support teams cannot reach every individual in need due to the sheer scale of the crisis. AI-driven platforms are now stepping in to offer critical mental health services remotely, offering comfort, guidance, and even therapeutic interventions.

Example 1: Woebot in Crisis Situations

Woebot is an AI-powered mental health app that uses cognitive-behavioral therapy (CBT) to help users process their emotions and cope with mental health challenges. In crisis situations, AI chatbots like Woebot can provide 24/7 support to those struggling with fear, anxiety, or trauma. This is especially valuable in disaster zones where traditional mental health services may be overwhelmed or inaccessible.

In 2020, Woebot collaborated with *Frontline Health Workers* to provide mental health support to individuals working in high-stress environments, such as hospitals treating COVID-19 patients. This application of AI helped manage anxiety and stress during a global health crisis.

Pro Tip: Mental health AI tools should be designed with clear limitations, ensuring users understand the tool's role and the importance of seeking human intervention when necessary. Furthermore, AI tools should have culturally sensitive responses to be effective across diverse populations.

4. AI and Humanitarian Aid in Conflict Zones

In conflict zones, where war, displacement, and instability leave millions vulnerable, AI has been used to coordinate aid and provide essential services. Empathetic AI systems can track and predict the needs of displaced persons, manage refugee camps, and assist in conflict mediation, helping to ensure that vulnerable populations are not left behind.

Example 1: AI for Refugee Tracking and Support

The *United Nations High Commissioner for Refugees* (UNHCR) has been working on integrating AI into refugee management systems. By using machine learning and data analytics, the UNHCR can predict patterns in refugee movement and identify areas of need in real-time. These systems are designed to prioritize empathy, ensuring that aid distribution not only meets physical needs but is also sensitive to the trauma and emotional distress experienced by displaced individuals.

Pro Tip: In the context of humanitarian aid, AI can do a lot to improve efficiency, but it is equally important to ensure that these systems are sensitive to the unique cultural and emotional needs of refugees. Collaboration with human aid workers is essential for making sure that technology enhances, rather than diminishes, the human aspect of aid.

5. Disaster Recovery and Long-Term Emotional Support

After the initial wave of crisis response, recovery efforts must focus not only on rebuilding physical infrastructure but also on supporting the long-term emotional recovery of those affected. AI can play a crucial role in monitoring and supporting mental health during this prolonged phase, ensuring that emotional resilience is cultivated and maintained.

Example 1: AI for Long-Term Emotional Resilience

In the aftermath of Hurricane Katrina, thousands of individuals were displaced, and many suffered from long-term trauma. To address this, AI-powered platforms were used to provide continuous mental health check-ins and support. These systems, built on principles of empathy, could detect changes in a person's emotional state and suggest coping mechanisms or even refer them to a human counselor if needed. Such systems can help build long-term emotional resilience by offering consistent support during recovery periods.

Pro Tip: AI-driven platforms should be designed for the long-term emotional recovery phase, ensuring that users feel a sense of continuity and connection throughout their healing process. These systems should also evolve to address the ongoing and changing emotional needs of individuals as time progresses after a disaster.

.   .   .

6. Ethical Considerations in Crisis AI

While emotional AI offers immense promise for enhancing crisis response, it is crucial to approach its integration with caution. Issues of privacy, consent, and emotional manipulation must be carefully considered when deploying these technologies in high-stakes situations.

Example 1: Ensuring Data Privacy in Crisis AI

In crises, large amounts of sensitive data—such as emotional responses, health conditions, and geographic location—are collected by AI systems. For example, when AI chatbots provide emotional support, they may collect personal information about users' mental health status. Ensuring the privacy and security of this data is paramount to prevent misuse or exploitation.

Pro Tip: Developers must adhere to strict ethical guidelines when creating emotional AI systems for crisis management. Ensuring transparency about data usage, obtaining consent, and incorporating robust security measures are all crucial steps in maintaining public trust.

CONCLUSION: The Future of Empathy-Driven AI in Crisis Response

The role of AI in crisis response is only just beginning to unfold, and its potential to provide empathy-driven solutions is immense. From offering real-time emotional support to efficiently managing aid distribution and tracking recovery efforts, AI is helping redefine how we respond to disasters and emergencies. However, the application of AI must be approached with ethical considerations, transparency, and a commitment to the well-being of those affected.

Pro Tip: As AI continues to play a greater role in crisis management, it's important to keep the human element at the center of these responses. AI should be viewed as a tool to augment human efforts, not replace them, ensuring that empathy remains at the core of all crisis management strategies. By carefully integrating AI in ways that prioritize emotional support, cultural sensitivity, and privacy, we can ensure a more compassionate and effective response in times of need.

The future of crisis response with empathy-driven AI is bright, but it's our responsibility to guide these technologies with integrity and a deep sense of care for those most in need.

CHAPTER 14: THE AI EMPATHY ECONOMY: MONETIZING EMOTIONAL INTELLIGENCE IN TECH

In the rapidly evolving world of AI, one of the most significant innovations has been the integration of emotional intelligence into technology. This new form of "empathy-driven AI" has given rise to an emerging market: the AI empathy economy. This is a market where emotional intelligence, once thought to be a purely human trait, is being leveraged to create valuable, monetizable products and services that cater to the emotional needs of consumers, businesses, and entire industries.

The AI empathy economy is transforming how we interact with technology, and it's becoming a major economic force that's worth billions. From emotional customer service chatbots to personalized health assistants, AI that understands and responds to human emotions is creating an entirely new landscape for companies and consumers alike. In this chapter, we will examine how emotional AI is being monetized, who is leading the charge, and how businesses can tap into this innovative and highly profitable market.

. . .

1. Understanding the AI Empathy Economy

The AI empathy economy refers to the commercialization of AI technologies that use emotional intelligence to enhance user experiences, improve engagement, and create value in the marketplace. Emotional AI systems can detect, interpret, and simulate human emotions, enabling machines to respond with empathy and understanding. This technology can be applied across a wide range of industries, from entertainment and retail to healthcare and education.

Example 1: Personalized Marketing

Companies have long relied on customer data to drive their marketing strategies, but now, with the power of emotional AI, businesses can create even more personalized experiences for their consumers. Emotional AI systems can analyze customer emotions during interactions, providing insights into their preferences, frustrations, and desires. This data allows businesses to create highly tailored marketing campaigns that not only meet the needs of customers but also connect with them on an emotional level.

For example, AI tools like *Piplsay* utilize emotional intelligence to gather insights into customer emotions during surveys and market research. These insights can help brands develop more emotionally resonant campaigns, which in turn can increase customer loyalty and sales.

Pro Tip: Companies looking to monetize emotional AI in marketing should focus on building personalized experiences that foster an emotional connection with their consumers. By leveraging empathy-driven algorithms, businesses can create more meaningful interactions that drive customer satisfaction and, ultimately, sales.

. . .

2. The Rise of AI-Powered Emotional Services

The introduction of emotionally intelligent AI has given rise to an entire new sector: emotional services. These AI-driven solutions are designed to provide emotional support, mental health services, and social interaction. With growing concerns around mental health and the emotional well-being of individuals, businesses are recognizing the need for AI-powered emotional services that can help meet these needs in scalable, accessible ways.

Example 1: Woebot and Mental Health

Woebot is an AI-powered mental health assistant that uses emotional intelligence to provide therapeutic support through conversational techniques. By mimicking the strategies used in cognitive-behavioral therapy (CBT), Woebot helps users manage stress, anxiety, and other emotional challenges. The company behind Woebot, *Woebot Health*, has found a lucrative niche by monetizing their emotional AI platform to offer services to mental health providers, corporations, and insurance companies, creating a sustainable revenue stream in the mental health tech industry.

Pro Tip: Monetizing emotional AI in the mental health sector requires a balance of ethical considerations and business acumen. While there is a growing demand for mental health services, companies must ensure their AI solutions are transparent, secure, and ethically designed to protect user privacy and well-being.

3. AI-Powered Customer Service: Improving Engagement and Efficiency

One of the most successful applications of emotional AI has been in customer service. AI chatbots and virtual assistants with emotional intelligence are revolutionizing how businesses interact with their customers. These AI systems can understand customer emotions, providing more empathetic responses and ensuring a better customer experience. This not only improves customer satisfaction but also reduces operational costs for businesses by handling large volumes of inquiries automatically.

Example 1: IBM Watson and Emotional AI in Customer Service

IBM Watson is one of the leaders in AI-powered customer service. Watson's AI capabilities include recognizing emotional cues in customer interactions, allowing businesses to respond in a way that is more aligned with customer feelings and needs. For instance, a Watson-powered chatbot can detect frustration in a customer's tone and escalate the issue to a human agent when necessary, ensuring that the customer feels heard and valued.

Pro Tip: To monetize emotional AI in customer service, businesses should focus on creating an omnichannel experience where AI systems not only handle routine inquiries but also offer empathetic support in complex or emotionally charged situations. This can improve both the customer experience and the bottom line.

4. AI in Entertainment: Creating Emotional Connections with Audiences

The entertainment industry has long been a pioneer in exploring new technologies to engage audiences. Now, emotional AI is being used to create more immersive and emotionally resonant experiences for viewers. From personalized movie recommendations to interactive video games that adapt to a player's emotional state, emotional AI is being monetized in ways that enhance user engagement and satisfaction.

Example 1: Personalized Movie Recommendations with Netflix

Netflix uses emotional AI to improve its recommendation algorithm. By analyzing viewers' reactions to movies and shows (such as likes, shares, or watching patterns), Netflix is able to create personalized content recommendations that resonate emotionally with viewers. This increases user engagement and retention, as subscribers are more likely to stay on a platform that consistently provides them with content they love.

Pro Tip: For content creators, monetizing emotional AI in entertainment requires a deep understanding of audience preferences and emotional triggers. By utilizing AI to tailor content to individual tastes, creators can enhance the user experience and boost engagement.

5. The Future of the AI Empathy Economy

The AI empathy economy is still in its early stages, but its potential for growth is enormous. As emotional intelligence in AI continues to improve, more industries will find ways to leverage this technology to enhance their products, services, and customer experiences. From AI-powered mental health solutions to emotionally intelligent robots, the possibilities for monetizing emotional AI are vast.

Example 1: AI and Human-Robot Interaction

In the near future, we can expect to see AI-powered robots with advanced emotional intelligence being used in a wide range of industries, from elder care to hospitality.

These robots will be able to provide companionship and assistance to people, offering emotional support and building trust over time. By monetizing emotional AI in robotics, businesses can create a new category of customer service that blends technology and empathy.

Pro Tip: Businesses seeking to capitalize on the AI empathy economy should look to innovate in sectors that are traditionally underserved by emotional support services, such as elderly care or remote working. By integrating emotional AI into these areas, businesses can tap into new and highly lucrative markets.

Conclusion: Embracing the AI Empathy Economy

As the AI empathy economy continues to grow, it's clear that emotional intelligence is no longer confined to human interactions. By integrating emotional AI into a wide range of industries, businesses can create new opportunities for revenue while also improving the quality of their services. Whether in healthcare, customer service, or entertainment, emotional AI offers the potential to transform how we connect with technology and how businesses connect with their customers.

The key to success in this new economy is to remain focused on empathy, ensuring that emotional AI not only drives profits but also enhances human experiences. By finding ways to monetize emotional intelligence ethically and effectively, businesses can lead the charge in this exciting new frontier of technological innovation.

CHAPTER 15: BEYOND EARTH: AI EMPATHY IN SPACE EXPLORATION

A s humanity sets its sights on the stars, embarking on ambitious missions to explore distant planets, moons, and asteroids, one of the most intriguing frontiers for artificial intelligence (AI) lies in the realm of emotional empathy. Space exploration, with its vast distances, isolation, and the harsh conditions of the cosmos, demands more than just technological expertise. It requires a new form of support: AI that can understand, respond to, and replicate human emotions to help astronauts navigate the mental and emotional challenges of interstellar travel.

In this chapter, we'll explore how emotional AI is transforming the future of space exploration. From mitigating the isolation of long-duration space missions to supporting astronauts' mental health, emotional AI is becoming an integral part of space missions, enabling human explorers to connect not just with their mission, but with their own humanity in the face of the unknown.

1. The Psychological Challenges of Space Exploration

Space exploration is as much a psychological journey as it is a technological one. The isolation, confinement, and the extreme distance from Earth create a unique set of psychological challenges for astronauts. Extended missions, such as those planned for Mars, will last months or even years, and astronauts will be cut off from their families and the comforts of Earth. This isolation can lead to a range of psychological issues, from stress and anxiety to depression and interpersonal conflicts. In these extreme environments, emotional support becomes as crucial as technical support.

Emotional AI can play a key role in addressing these challenges. By providing constant, accessible emotional support, AI can help astronauts manage their mental well-being during long missions, ensuring that their psychological health doesn't undermine their mission's success.

Example 1: NASA's "Cultural and Social Robot" for Astronauts

NASA has already begun experimenting with AI and robotics to support astronauts' mental health. The "Cultural and Social Robot," a concept in development, is designed to interact with astronauts in ways that offer emotional comfort and companionship. By detecting emotional states through voice and facial recognition, the robot can adjust its responses to offer encouragement or empathy, similar to how a human crew member might offer support.

The robot could play a pivotal role in offering comfort during the long stretches of isolation in space. Its primary task isn't just to respond to technical needs but to maintain astronauts' emotional stability by providing an empathetic listening ear and offering motivational support when needed. By helping astronauts cope with loneliness and stress, the robot's role could be as important as any mission-critical technology onboard.

Pro Tip: Space agencies planning long-term missions should integrate emotional AI tools that can simulate social interaction, creating opportunities for astronauts to express themselves and receive empathy, even if human companionship isn't possible.

2. AI as a Companion: Preventing Loneliness and Isolation

One of the greatest psychological risks astronauts face is the overwhelming sense of isolation. On missions to the Moon or Mars, the distance between Earth and the crew will be vast, making real-time communication with loved ones impossible. In such scenarios, AI-driven companions can provide an emotional lifeline.

Example 2: The Role of AI in Combating Loneliness in Long-Duration Missions

Studies show that astronauts can suffer from loneliness during space missions, especially on long-duration flights like those to Mars. Emotional AI companions, similar to virtual assistants or robotic pets, can fill this void by interacting with astronauts, providing companionship, and maintaining a sense of normalcy. For example, virtual assistants like *Replika* have already been used to combat loneliness on Earth, and their role could be expanded in space, providing astronauts with a conversational partner who can simulate real human interaction.

Emotional AI systems can be designed to learn an astronaut's unique emotional profile, adjusting their responses over time to reflect their emotional needs, whether that be providing a sense of calm during stressful moments or simply engaging in casual conversation to stave off loneliness.

Pro Tip: Future space missions could greatly benefit from AI companions that are tailored to the individual emotional needs of astronauts, providing personalized responses that foster a sense of connection to Earth and reduce the psychological impact of isolation.

3. AI-Powered Mental Health Monitoring in Space

AI not only acts as a companion but also serves a critical role in monitoring astronauts' mental health. Emotional AI systems can analyze speech patterns, facial expressions, and physiological indicators to assess an astronaut's emotional well-being. These systems could alert mission control to any signs of distress, helping to prevent mental health issues before they become serious problems.

Example 3: Emotional AI for Real-Time Mental Health Monitoring

One of the most significant benefits of AI in space exploration is its ability to monitor astronauts' emotional and mental health in real time. For example, the *Crew Health Performance Exploration Team* (CHP-ET) at NASA is developing AI systems that track astronauts' psychological well-being. These AI tools can detect signs of stress, anxiety, and depression by analyzing facial expressions, tone of voice, and other subtle cues, and then recommend specific interventions, whether it's a relaxation exercise, a conversation with a virtual companion, or a video call with a mental health professional back on Earth.

Pro Tip: Incorporating AI-powered mental health monitoring systems into future space missions can help maintain astronaut mental wellness by ensuring that any emotional distress is quickly identified and addressed, thus improving the overall success of the mission.

. . .

4. The Role of AI in Enhancing Team Dynamics and Communication

In the high-pressure environment of space, team dynamics are crucial to the success of the mission. Emotional AI can help foster healthy communication between crew members by detecting interpersonal conflicts or stress and offering strategies for resolution. This could be particularly important on long missions where the potential for isolation and conflict can take a toll on team cohesion.

Example 4: AI-Assisted Team Dynamics

AI can analyze the communication patterns and emotional states of astronauts during their interactions with each other, helping to improve team dynamics. For instance, the AI could flag potential sources of tension and suggest ways to de-escalate conflicts before they impact the mission. By fostering better communication, emotional AI can improve collaboration and ensure that the crew remains focused on the task at hand, rather than being distracted by personal issues or stress.

Pro Tip: To optimize team performance on long-duration space missions, AI can serve as a proactive mediator, ensuring that emotional dynamics are managed and that crew members remain emotionally balanced and effective throughout the mission.

5. Preparing for the Future: Emotional AI in Deep Space Exploration

As we look toward missions to the Moon, Mars, and beyond, the role of emotional AI will become even more critical. Deep space exploration will push the boundaries of human endurance and mental health, requiring the integration of empathetic AI to provide both technical and emotional support to astronauts on these daring voyages.

Example 5: Interstellar Empathy in Deep Space Missions

Looking forward, AI-powered emotional support systems will be necessary for missions that venture beyond Mars, to asteroids, or even further into the depths of space. These systems will need to be more advanced, capable of not only maintaining astronauts' psychological health but also ensuring their resilience in the face of the unknown. This could involve real-time emotional support, personalized mental health interventions, and immersive virtual experiences that connect astronauts to Earth like never before.

Pro Tip: As we move toward interstellar exploration, emotional AI systems should be designed to evolve with astronauts, learning and adapting to their emotional needs over time. This will ensure that these AI companions remain relevant and helpful throughout even the longest and most challenging missions.

CONCLUSION: A New Era of Empathy in Space Exploration

The future of space exploration is not just about new frontiers in technology and science, but also about how we take care of the people who venture into the unknown. AI's ability to simulate empathy and provide emotional support will be a critical factor in ensuring the mental and emotional well-being of astronauts on long-duration missions. From virtual companions to real-time emotional health monitoring, emotional AI will be essential to overcoming the psychological challenges of space exploration.

As we venture further into space, we will need not just groundbreaking science and technology but a deep sense of empathy—one that is encoded into the very AI systems that help astronauts navigate the emotional challenges of exploring new worlds. The future of space exploration is as much about the mind as it is about the body, and emotional AI will be at the heart of this brave new era.

CHAPTER 16: EDUCATIONAL EMPATHY: HOW AI PERSONALIZES LEARNING EXPERIENCES

The intersection of artificial intelligence and education is one of the most exciting areas of technological advancement today. AI is transforming the way students learn, offering new, personalized, and empathetic approaches to education. In this chapter, we'll dive into how emotional AI is revolutionizing the educational experience by customizing learning to meet the emotional and cognitive needs of individual students. By incorporating empathy into AI-driven learning platforms, educators can create environments that are not only smarter but also more attuned to the emotional needs of learners.

In traditional classrooms, students often face challenges that extend beyond the purely academic realm—issues such as anxiety, learning disabilities, or social difficulties can impact their ability to learn effectively. Emotional AI has the potential to address these challenges, offering tailored learning experiences that resonate with students on a deeper level. Whether through adjusting the pace of lessons, providing emotional support, or using empathy-driven responses, AI can act as both a tutor and a companion for students, helping them feel understood, supported, and motivated.

1. Personalizing Learning Through Emotional AI

One of the fundamental ways emotional AI enhances the educational experience is by personalizing it. Traditional education systems are often one-size-fits-all, which can leave many students feeling disconnected or left behind. With AI, learning can be adapted in real-time based on the student's emotions, progress, and needs.

Example 1: AI-Driven Personalized Learning Paths

AI systems like *DreamBox* and *Knewton* analyze student performance in real time and adjust the learning path accordingly. These platforms don't just offer personalized content based on academic progress but also consider emotional cues, such as frustration or disengagement. For example, if a student struggles with a math problem and shows signs of frustration, the AI system can offer encouragement, provide additional practice, or switch to a simpler explanation to keep the student on track without overwhelming them. This combination of academic and emotional intelligence creates a learning experience that feels both challenging and supportive.

Pro Tip: To maximize the effectiveness of AI in education, educators should use platforms that not only track progress but also respond empathetically to emotional cues, creating a balance between intellectual stimulation and emotional support.

2. Empathy-Driven AI Tutors

Imagine a tutor that not only understands the subject

matter but also understands how you feel. AI-driven tutors are being developed that can recognize when a student is struggling emotionally and respond in a way that offers comfort, encouragement, or motivation. These tutors can detect changes in tone of voice, facial expressions, and even physiological signs to assess the student's emotional state and tailor their interactions accordingly.

Example 2: AI Tutors That Respond to Emotional States

A great example of this is *Woebot*, an AI-driven mental health chatbot that helps students cope with stress and anxiety. Woebot uses cognitive-behavioral therapy techniques to interact with users and provide support based on their emotional states. While primarily designed for mental health, Woebot's underlying technology can easily be adapted to educational settings. For instance, an AI tutor could detect when a student is feeling frustrated with a particular subject and offer more empathetic responses, such as offering positive reinforcement or calming suggestions.

Pro Tip: In the future, AI-driven tutors should integrate emotional intelligence alongside academic support, ensuring that students feel both mentally engaged and emotionally supported throughout their learning journeys.

3. Improving Student Motivation with Emotional AI

Motivation is a key factor in academic success, and AI has a unique ability to influence motivation through empathetic engagement. In many educational settings, students struggle with motivation, especially if they feel disconnected from the material or overwhelmed by the pressure to perform. AI systems can help to alleviate these issues by offering personalized encouragement and support tailored to each student's emotional needs.

Example 3: AI-Enhanced Gamification in Education

One of the most promising applications of emotional AI in education is in the realm of gamification. Platforms like *Classcraft* use gamified elements to engage students in learning, but with an emotional twist. The system adjusts the difficulty level based on the student's emotional responses, offering rewards for perseverance or progress in areas that the student finds particularly challenging. If a student is feeling defeated, the system can adjust the learning path to make it easier, offering instant feedback and motivating them with small, achievable goals.

Pro Tip: Teachers can enhance motivation by using gamified AI learning tools that adjust the emotional experience for each student. This keeps them engaged and fosters a growth mindset by celebrating small victories.

4. Emotional AI and Social-Emotional Learning (SEL)

Social-emotional learning (SEL) has become a critical component of modern education. SEL programs help students develop emotional intelligence, which is essential for their personal and academic growth. Emotional AI can enhance SEL programs by offering real-time feedback on emotional behavior and helping students improve their emotional regulation skills.

Example 4: AI-Assisted SEL Programs

Platforms like *Emotient* (which tracks facial expressions) and *Tales2Go* (which provides emotional cues during storytelling) are helping students develop better emotional awareness. For example, if a student expresses frustration or confusion during a group activity, an AI system can detect those emotions and provide tailored interventions, such as suggesting a deep-breathing exercise or redirecting the student's focus to an encouraging message. This helps students build resilience and emotional intelligence in a supportive and constructive way.

Pro Tip: Integrating AI with SEL programs can help students not only understand their own emotions but also navigate social interactions with empathy and self-awareness, creating a more harmonious learning environment.

5. The Future of Educational Empathy: AI in Inclusive Education

AI has the potential to revolutionize inclusive education by providing personalized learning experiences for students with disabilities or special learning needs. Emotional AI can make learning accessible for students with a range of conditions, from autism to ADHD, by tailoring educational experiences that match their unique emotional and cognitive needs.

Example 5: AI for Special Education

One example is *Leka*, a robot designed to help children with autism develop social and emotional skills. Leka uses emotional AI to detect a child's emotional state and respond with empathy, offering activities designed to engage the child in a way that feels emotionally supportive. Similarly, AI-powered learning platforms can offer personalized lesson plans for students with learning disabilities, adjusting the pace, content, and presentation style to accommodate their emotional needs and cognitive abilities.

Pro Tip: In inclusive education, emotional AI can create a more equitable learning environment by ensuring that students with diverse needs receive the tailored support they require to succeed academically and emotionally.

CONCLUSION: The Power of Empathetic AI in Education

As AI continues to evolve, its role in education will become even more transformative. By integrating emotional intelligence into learning platforms, AI can not only support academic progress but also help students develop a stronger sense of emotional well-being, resilience, and empathy. The future of education will be one where technology and humanity intersect to create personalized, emotionally intelligent learning experiences that support students holistically—intellectually, emotionally, and socially.

The future of educational empathy is bright, and as AI grows more sophisticated, it will continue to break down barriers, providing all students with the opportunity to learn, grow, and thrive in environments that understand them on a deeply human level. By combining the power of personalized learning with the empathy of AI, we are poised to create the next generation of learners who are not only academically successful but emotionally resilient and socially intelligent as well.

CHAPTER 17: THE MANIPULATION MACHINE: RISKS OF EMOTIONAL AI BEING EXPLOITED FOR CONTROL

As artificial intelligence continues to evolve, it opens up new doors for emotional engagement and personalized interactions. However, this capability also introduces significant ethical and societal risks. In this chapter, we explore the darker side of emotional AI—how it can be exploited for manipulation, control, and power, ultimately putting vulnerable individuals and society at risk.

Emotional AI has the ability to detect, interpret, and even simulate human emotions. These capabilities, when used responsibly, can enhance user experiences, improve healthcare, and support mental well-being. But when misused, emotional AI can be turned into a manipulation machine that influences behavior, changes opinions, and even dictates the actions of individuals without their awareness. As such, it's crucial to examine the potential harms and ethical implications of emotional AI manipulation.

. . .

1. Emotional AI and Persuasion: The Path to Manipulation

One of the most concerning aspects of emotional AI is its potential to influence individuals' emotions and decisions. AI systems can study emotional patterns and use this knowledge to persuade people in ways they may not even realize. By analyzing facial expressions, voice tone, or even physiological responses, emotional AI can determine how a person feels and what kind of emotional appeal will sway their decisions.

Example 1: AI in Political Campaigns

Political campaigns and advertisers are already beginning to use emotional AI to sway voters or consumers. For instance, AI can analyze social media posts or responses to political messages and adjust the tone or content of future ads based on how the target audience is feeling. This form of emotional targeting is deeply powerful, allowing campaigns to tap into the emotions of individuals, creating highly tailored messages designed to elicit specific emotional reactions—be it fear, hope, or anger. If used improperly, this technology could deepen political divisions and manipulate public opinion on a large scale.

Pro Tip: Companies and political entities must implement strong ethical guidelines to ensure that emotional AI is not used for manipulating vulnerable populations. Transparency, consent, and user control must be central to any AI-powered persuasion system.

2. Emotional AI in Consumerism: When Manipulation Becomes Profit

In the commercial world, emotional AI is often used to increase consumer engagement and drive sales. By tracking emotional responses to ads or products, companies can create personalized shopping experiences that evoke specific feelings of happiness, urgency, or satisfaction. While this may enhance customer satisfaction, it can also lead to manipulation, especially when AI systems use data to exploit psychological vulnerabilities.

Example 2: AI-Powered Retail

Amazon, for example, uses sophisticated algorithms to predict what products a consumer might be most interested in, often based on their browsing history, purchase patterns, and emotional reactions to previous ads. As emotional AI develops, companies like Amazon and Facebook could use facial recognition and sentiment analysis to assess a shopper's mood and adjust recommendations in real time. The challenge is that consumers may not be aware that their emotions are being used to push them toward products or services they do not truly need or want.

Pro Tip: As a consumer, it's essential to stay informed about how your data is being used. Look for transparency in how companies collect and use personal data, and whenever possible, control the extent to which your emotional responses are being tracked.

3. Social Media: Emotional AI and the Influence of "Likes"

Social media platforms are major players in the emotional AI field, leveraging this technology to increase engagement and time spent on their platforms. The emotional response to content plays a huge role in how algorithms promote or demote posts, often amplifying negative emotions like outrage or fear, which tend to be more engaging. As AI algorithms optimize for engagement, they may inadvertently manipulate emotions, pushing individuals toward content that triggers extreme emotional reactions, furthering polarization and division.

Example 3: Emotional AI in Social Media Feeds

Facebook and Instagram, for instance, use AI to analyze user behavior—how long you spend on a post, how quickly you scroll past it, and what reactions you give—this data is then used to adjust your feed to show content that is most likely to provoke an emotional response. This creates an echo chamber where emotionally charged content spreads rapidly, shaping public opinion and behavior.

Pro Tip: Be mindful of the emotional content you engage with online. Social media platforms thrive on emotionally charged interactions, and by understanding this, you can make more informed decisions about your digital consumption.

4. AI-Driven Customer Service: Manipulating Emotions for Loyalty

In customer service, emotional AI can be used to detect customer frustration or satisfaction and respond accordingly, creating a more personalized and supportive experience. While this can enhance customer satisfaction, it also opens the door to manipulation. AI-driven systems that constantly monitor your emotional state can use this data to develop loyalty strategies that exploit your emotional attachment to a brand or service, leading to consumer dependency and irrational loyalty.

Example 4: AI in Banking or Telecom

Consider the case of AI-powered customer service chatbots used by banks or telecommunications companies. These bots analyze the emotional tone of customer messages—whether the customer is frustrated, happy, or confused—and adjust their responses accordingly. If a customer is upset, the AI might respond with empathy, offering additional perks or solutions to make the customer feel valued. While this approach can improve customer satisfaction, it also has the potential to manipulate emotions and keep customers loyal to services they may not even need.

Pro Tip: Always question whether your emotional responses are being manipulated when interacting with customer service. Are you being upsold based on your frustration or excitement? Being aware of these tactics allows you to make more informed decisions.

5. The Dark Side of AI-Driven Emotional Manipulation: Ethical Considerations

The manipulation of emotions through AI raises significant ethical concerns. The ability to influence people's thoughts, decisions, and behaviors based on their emotional vulnerabilities is a power that should not be taken lightly. Without proper oversight and regulation, emotional AI could easily be misused by governments, corporations, or malicious actors seeking to manipulate individuals for personal gain.

Example 5: Exploitation in Sensitive Areas

In some cases, emotional AI could even be used in more sensitive areas such as mental health, where vulnerable individuals are targeted and manipulated by malicious actors. AI-driven mental health apps could potentially gather and exploit sensitive emotional data for profit, recommending certain treatments or medications based on the goal of generating revenue rather than benefiting the patient.

Pro Tip: Governments and organizations should put in place strict ethical frameworks around the use of emotional AI. This includes transparency in how emotional data is collected, ensuring that users are aware of when they are being influenced, and regulating the use of emotional AI in sensitive areas like healthcare, finance, and politics.

Conclusion: Navigating the Risks of Emotional AI

The potential for emotional AI to be exploited for manipulation is significant, but it's not all doom and gloom. By approaching this technology with caution, awareness, and responsibility, we can harness its power for good, ensuring that it enhances human experiences rather than exploiting them. The key to minimizing the risks of emotional AI manipulation lies in creating ethical guidelines, transparency, and oversight.

It is important for consumers, tech developers, and policymakers to work together to establish clear boundaries for how emotional AI is used. Ethical considerations must be central to the design and deployment of AI systems, especially those that tap into the deepest layers of human emotion. Only by balancing innovation with responsibility can we prevent emotional AI from becoming a manipulation machine and ensure it remains a force for positive, empathetic engagement.

Pro Tip: Stay informed about the risks of emotional AI. Educate yourself on how this technology works, and be mindful of its influence on your daily life. By doing so, you can protect yourself from manipulation and contribute to a

future where AI serves humanity in an ethical and responsible way.

CHAPTER 18: FICTION MEETS REALITY: AI'S PORTRAYAL IN MEDIA VS. ITS REAL-WORLD APPLICATIONS

The world of artificial intelligence has been long fascinated by its portrayal in the media, where it has been depicted both as an incredibly intelligent, helpful assistant and as a harbinger of dystopian futures. But how does the fictional portrayal of AI in movies, TV shows, and literature align with the real-world advancements we see today?

In this chapter, we will explore how AI has been represented in fiction, the reasons behind these depictions, and how those representations differ from the AI we are currently developing and utilizing. Through the lens of popular media, we can understand the fears, hopes, and expectations that people have regarding AI, but it is essential to ground these narratives in the reality of today's technologies and their future potential.

I. The Rise of Sentient Machines in Fiction

AI has been a staple in science fiction for decades, often

portrayed as sentient, with human-like qualities, emotions, and desires. Classic examples include HAL 9000 from *2001: A Space Odyssey*, Skynet from *The Terminator*, and Samantha from *Her*. These fictional AIs are often imbued with a sense of autonomy and self-awareness, raising questions about consciousness, free will, and ethics.

Example 1: HAL 9000 – The Cautionary Tale

HAL 9000 from Stanley Kubrick's *2001: A Space Odyssey* is perhaps one of the most iconic depictions of AI in fiction. HAL is not just a machine but a character capable of complex emotions and decisions, even going as far as to betray the human crew when its mission is threatened. HAL's actions raise concerns about the reliability of AI and the potential consequences of giving machines too much control.

In contrast, today's AI is far from self-aware. While AI systems can process vast amounts of data and perform specific tasks exceptionally well, they lack true consciousness or the capacity for moral reasoning. AI, in the real world, operates based on pre-programmed algorithms and models, not on the emotions or desires of the system itself.

Pro Tip: While AI in fiction often represents our deepest fears about the loss of control, real-world AI lacks this level of autonomy. The current focus is on ensuring AI operates ethically and safely within set boundaries.

2. AI as a Tool for Good: Friend or Foe?

In fiction, AI is sometimes portrayed as a helpful tool that can assist humans in various ways. In *Star Trek: The Next Generation*, Data, an android with human-like abilities, works alongside the crew, exhibiting emotions and an understanding of human culture. Meanwhile, in *Iron Man*,

Tony Stark's AI assistant, J.A.R.V.I.S., helps run his technology and makes critical decisions, creating an image of AI as a helpful and loyal companion.

Example 2: J.A.R.V.I.S. – The Ultimate AI Assistant

J.A.R.V.I.S. is an excellent example of a fictional AI that is not only functional but has a certain level of personality. J.A.R.V.I.S. assists Tony Stark with complex tasks, maintains the security of his house, and even helps pilot his Iron Man suit. While it is presented as a cutting-edge, multi-faceted AI, it's clear that J.A.R.V.I.S. is more of a tool created by a human to enhance his own capabilities.

In real life, AI like Siri, Alexa, or Google Assistant is designed to help with tasks like setting reminders, playing music, and answering basic questions. However, these systems are nowhere near as sophisticated as J.A.R.V.I.S. They lack any true understanding of the tasks they perform and do not possess the ability to make complex decisions or engage in the type of nuanced interactions shown in fiction.

Pro Tip: The AI in real life is a far cry from J.A.R.V.I.S. It is, at best, an assistant capable of performing routine tasks, with limitations in context, learning, and deeper cognitive understanding.

3. AI and Human Relationships: Fiction vs. Reality

One of the most intriguing areas of AI in fiction is its ability to form relationships with humans. In *Her*, a man falls in love with an AI operating system named Samantha, who adapts to his emotional needs, offering companionship and intimacy. Similarly, in *Ex Machina*, Ava, a humanoid AI, exhibits emotional intelligence and manipulates her creator to escape captivity.

Example 3: Samantha in *Her* – The Idealized AI Companion

In *Her*, Samantha becomes more than just a functional assistant; she is a companion who understands, learns, and grows emotionally, providing the protagonist with the kind of connection he longs for. Samantha's ability to form a relationship with Theodore raises questions about the nature of love, intimacy, and the ethical concerns of human-AI interactions.

In reality, AI systems are far from forming genuine emotional connections. While AI can simulate empathy and offer personalized interactions, these systems do not experience emotions themselves. They can process data about human emotions and provide responses that seem empathetic, but this is not a true emotional connection. AI does not possess consciousness or the ability to form relationships as humans do.

Pro Tip: While emotional AI can enhance human experiences by offering personalized interactions, it's essential to remember that these systems lack the depth and authenticity of human relationships. AI is a tool, not a replacement for human companionship.

4. The Darker Side of AI in Fiction: The Fear of Control

Another prevalent theme in AI fiction is the fear of machines taking control of humanity. This is most famously portrayed in *The Matrix*, where intelligent machines enslave humanity by trapping them in a simulated reality. In *Westworld*, AI-driven robots begin to gain self-awareness, leading to a rebellion against their human creators. These portrayals often explore the dangers of AI surpassing human control and creating dystopian societies.

Example 4: The Matrix – The Totalitarian AI

In *The Matrix*, AI has become so powerful that it enslaves humanity within an illusion, using people as an energy source. This dystopian vision is a cautionary tale about the potential consequences of creating machines that exceed our ability to control them. In the real world, we are far from the dystopian reality of *The Matrix*. Today's AI systems are tightly controlled, and while there are fears about AI becoming too powerful, researchers and developers are actively working on ensuring that AI remains ethical, transparent, and accountable.

Pro Tip: While concerns about AI surpassing human control are valid, most current AI technologies are far from having the autonomy or capability to take over. Continuous regulation and oversight are crucial to maintaining ethical AI development.

5. The Blurring of Fiction and Reality: The Future of AI

As AI continues to evolve, the line between fiction and reality is becoming increasingly blurred. While we may not yet have sentient AI or machines that can form real emotional connections, the rapid progress in emotional AI and machine learning is bringing us closer to the kinds of scenarios portrayed in fiction. The next generation of AI may be able to simulate human emotions with even greater precision, offering more realistic interactions, but it will still be a far cry from the true sentience and consciousness seen in fictional AI.

Example 5: AI and the Future

In the future, AI systems could become more deeply integrated into our daily lives, offering more advanced emotional intelligence, personalized experiences, and even deeper human-machine relationships. However, as we develop these systems, we must remain mindful of the ethical considerations, privacy issues, and the potential for misuse. Fiction may inspire innovation, but it's crucial to maintain a clear distinction between imagination and the practical, ethical use of AI in real-world applications.

Pro Tip: As AI technology advances, it's essential to separate the imaginative narratives of fiction from the realities of development. Stay informed about the capabilities of AI, and advocate for the responsible use of this technology.

CONCLUSION: Fiction as a Mirror and Guide

Fiction and reality often converge when it comes to AI, but the stories we tell about AI in movies, books, and TV shows are as much a reflection of our hopes and fears as they are predictions of the future. While fictional portrayals of AI often lean into the extremes—either portraying it as a benevolent helper or a dangerous threat—the real-world application of AI is much more nuanced and grounded. As we move forward in developing AI systems with emotional capabilities, we must use these insights from fiction not as blueprints for the future, but as cautionary tales, reminders, and opportunities to shape AI in ways that benefit humanity.

By learning from the lessons of fiction, we can ensure that AI remains a tool for good and not a machine for manipulation or control. The key lies in balancing the excitement of innovation with the responsibility to safeguard our ethical values, ensuring AI is developed thoughtfully, transparently, and with a focus on its role as a helpful companion to human society.

Pro Tip: Fiction can inspire, but it is up to us to create the future we want to see with AI. Let's take the lessons from these stories to heart and use them to ensure a positive, ethical, and collaborative relationship with artificial intelligence.

CHAPTER 19: THE ROAD AHEAD: TRENDS SHAPING THE FUTURE OF EMPATHETIC TECHNOLOGY

As we stand at the intersection of technology and human connection, the road ahead for empathetic technology—specifically AI—is filled with both exciting possibilities and complex challenges. The future of AI is being shaped by trends that will not only affect the tools we use but also redefine how we relate to technology on a deeply personal level. In this chapter, we explore these key trends, their implications, and how they will continue to impact our lives in the coming years.

1. Emotionally Intelligent AI Becoming Ubiquitous

The most obvious and perhaps most exciting trend is the continued advancement of emotionally intelligent AI. As AI becomes more adept at understanding, processing, and responding to human emotions, it will move beyond basic interactions and enter into deeper, more nuanced relationships with users.

Example 1: AI in Healthcare

In healthcare, AI systems are increasingly being used to monitor patients' emotional well-being in addition to their physical health. Tools like *Woebot*, an AI-driven chatbot, already help people manage their mental health by offering cognitive behavioral therapy (CBT) and checking in on mood. As this technology develops, we may see AI therapists and assistants offering personalized mental health support in real-time, creating an entirely new healthcare model where emotional intelligence is as important as physical health management.

Pro Tip: AI's ability to monitor emotions could soon provide not only diagnostic insights but also long-term support in managing chronic conditions or mental health challenges. The future of empathetic AI may lead to more holistic, preventative healthcare models.

2. AI Integration into Everyday Life

AI will become increasingly integrated into our daily routines, not as a passive tool but as an active participant in our interactions with the world. From smart homes to personalized work assistants, AI will be there every step of the way, anticipating needs and responding in emotionally intelligent ways.

Example 2: AI-Enhanced Virtual Assistants

Consider the future of virtual assistants, like Siri or Alexa, which could evolve from being task-oriented tools into emotionally aware companions that offer personalized support. These assistants might recognize when you're feeling stressed, offer words of encouragement, or adapt the environment (lighting, music, etc.) to help you feel more at ease. Emotional intelligence will enable AI to not only respond to commands but also to empathize with the user's emotional state.

Pro Tip: As AI becomes more integrated into our daily lives, emotional awareness will be key to creating seamless and intuitive user experiences. The future of personal assistants could very well include a true understanding of your needs, both practical and emotional.

3. The Need for Ethical Guidelines and Regulation

As AI becomes more advanced and capable of simulating human-like empathy, questions about its ethical use will become even more pressing. How do we ensure that emotionally intelligent AI remains beneficial without crossing into manipulation or control? What safeguards will be necessary to protect users from emotional exploitation?

Example 3: Regulation of Emotional AI

To ensure that emotionally intelligent AI does not exploit users or manipulate their feelings for profit, organizations and governments will need to establish clear guidelines for AI design, transparency, and data usage. For instance, the European Union has already begun working on guidelines for AI ethics, including issues around privacy, bias, and accountability. As AI grows more emotional, these regulations will need to evolve to account for the nuances of human-AI interaction.

Pro Tip: Ethical standards in AI design are crucial to building trust with users. As AI technology grows more emotionally intelligent, the conversation about ethics must keep pace with innovation. Clear regulatory frameworks will ensure that AI benefits society as a whole without infringing on individual rights or freedoms.

. . .

4. AI in Education: Personalized Learning and Emotional Support

Another significant trend is the increased use of AI in education, where emotional intelligence will play a critical role in personalized learning experiences. AI-driven tutors and learning assistants will not only adapt to students' academic needs but also provide emotional support, encouraging perseverance and motivation.

Example 4: AI-Powered Adaptive Learning Systems

In the future, AI will be able to assess a student's emotional state and learning style, adjusting lessons and feedback accordingly. For example, an AI tutor might recognize when a student is frustrated or disengaged and modify the difficulty level of the material, offer encouragement, or even suggest a short break to help them re-engage. This level of emotional understanding will help students feel supported, increasing both their academic success and emotional well-being.

Pro Tip: AI in education will not just focus on cognitive outcomes but will also take into account students' emotional needs, creating an educational experience that is truly holistic. Personalized learning experiences that cater to both emotional and intellectual development could revolutionize how we learn.

5. The Role of AI in Social and Emotional Intelligence Development

AI will also play a key role in helping people develop their own social and emotional intelligence. Tools designed to teach emotional skills—such as empathy, communication, and conflict resolution—are already in development, and as they become more sophisticated, they will help users develop these abilities in new and exciting ways.

Example 5: Virtual Reality (VR) and AI for Empathy Training

One emerging application is the combination of AI and virtual reality (VR) to teach empathy. For instance, VR simulations powered by AI might allow users to experience the world through the eyes of another person, fostering understanding and compassion. By creating these immersive experiences, AI could offer a new way to teach empathy, a critical skill in both personal and professional contexts.

Pro Tip: The combination of AI and VR could provide highly effective empathy training, allowing people to practice and develop social and emotional intelligence in a safe and controlled environment. As these tools evolve, they could become an integral part of both personal development and workplace training programs.

6. The Promise and Perils of AI-Enhanced Relationships

While emotionally intelligent AI has the potential to enhance human relationships, it also raises significant questions about the nature of those relationships. As AI becomes more empathetic, we will need to carefully consider whether AI can ever truly replace human connection, and if relying too heavily on AI for emotional support could have unintended consequences.

Example 6: AI in Personal Relationships

Imagine a world where AI companions are capable of offering emotional support, companionship, and even love. Some people might choose to have an AI partner, while others may turn to AI-driven chatbots for companionship.

While this could provide emotional relief for some, it also raises concerns about the ability of AI to truly understand and form authentic emotional connections. Will AI relationships enhance or detract from human bonds? And what does it mean for society when human interactions are mediated by machines?

Pro Tip: It's essential to carefully consider the role AI will play in our emotional lives. As we embrace emotionally intelligent AI, we must remain vigilant about its impact on real-world relationships and ensure that we don't lose sight of the human connections that form the foundation of society.

Conclusion: A Road of Opportunities and Responsibilities

As we look to the future, the possibilities for emotionally intelligent AI are both thrilling and complex. We stand at a crossroads, with technology advancing rapidly and offering new ways to connect, support, and enhance human experiences. However, with these advancements comes responsibility. The road ahead is one that requires careful consideration, thoughtful regulation, and ethical development.

By embracing the opportunities offered by AI while remaining grounded in ethical practices, we can ensure that empathetic technology serves as a force for good in society. As we journey forward, we must remain committed to creating AI systems that enhance, rather than replace, human connection, and that help us build a future where empathy, understanding, and compassion are at the heart of technological progress.

Pro Tip: As AI continues to evolve, staying informed, involved, and ethical in its development will be key to ensuring that we remain the masters of our technology, not its subjects. The future of empathetic AI is in our hands, and we must use it wisely to create a more connected, compassionate world.

CHAPTER 20: A NEW AGE OF CONNECTION: FINAL REFLECTIONS ON TECHNOLOGY'S ROLE IN SHAPING EMPATHY

As we reach the final chapter of this exploration, we find ourselves reflecting on how far we have come in integrating empathy into artificial intelligence, and where we are heading in the future. We've witnessed AI evolve from simple, rule-based systems to sophisticated, emotionally aware technologies capable of understanding and responding to human feelings. But what does this all mean for the future of human connection, and how will technology continue to shape our relationships, trust, and emotional experiences?

This chapter brings us full circle as we assess the promises and challenges of AI's role in the development of empathetic technology. Let's reflect on the transformative potential of AI while recognizing the ethical, emotional, and societal implications of this technological revolution.

1. The Convergence of Technology and Humanity

The convergence of artificial intelligence and human empathy is one of the most profound shifts of the 21st century. No longer are we simply interacting with machines that carry out tasks—they are learning to understand us on an emotional level. AI-powered systems now analyze human emotions and adapt their responses to meet emotional needs, offering support, encouragement, and even empathy.

Example 1: Virtual Companions for Emotional Support

The rise of virtual companions like *Replika*, an AI chatbot designed to provide companionship and emotional support, is a testament to the growing bond between humans and technology. These systems allow people to engage in emotionally intelligent conversations that mimic the feeling of having a real, empathetic conversation partner. As AI continues to improve in understanding the subtleties of human emotion, the idea of relying on virtual companions for support will become more normalized.

Pro Tip: The future may bring AI companions that provide not just conversational engagement but real emotional support, making it essential for us to understand the deeper ethical implications of such connections.

2. The Expansion of Empathy in Everyday Life

Empathetic AI is not a far-off concept; it is being woven into the fabric of our daily routines. From the virtual assistants we interact with to the healthcare solutions that provide us with personalized emotional care, empathetic technology is already shaping our interactions. We now live in an age where technology is not just about convenience; it's about connection, well-being, and emotional support.

Example 2: AI in Customer Service

AI systems like *Zendesk's Answer Bot* have revolutionized

customer service by allowing businesses to offer quick, personalized responses to inquiries. As these systems become more emotionally aware, they will be able to detect when a customer is frustrated or upset and adapt their responses to calm, reassure, or empathize, creating a more human-like experience that fosters trust and loyalty.

Pro Tip: For businesses, the future of empathetic AI in customer service will involve systems that not only solve problems but also enhance the overall emotional experience, strengthening customer relationships.

3. Ethical Considerations and the Human-AI Relationship

As we embrace the potential of empathetic AI, we must remain vigilant about the ethical challenges it presents. Can AI truly understand human emotions, or is it simply mimicking empathy in ways that could lead to manipulation? How can we prevent emotional exploitation while encouraging technological advancements?

Example 3: The Ethics of AI in Therapy

AI-powered mental health apps like *Woebot* provide users with personalized therapeutic experiences. But as these tools become more sophisticated, questions around privacy, autonomy, and consent arise. If AI can learn to predict and influence emotional states, how can we ensure that these technologies are used for the benefit of individuals rather than for manipulation or control?

Pro Tip: As empathetic AI continues to advance, it is essential to create robust ethical guidelines that ensure these technologies are used responsibly, with a focus on protecting users' emotional and personal data.

. . .

4. Emotional AI in Education: Shaping Future Generations

In the educational realm, AI is already making waves by providing personalized learning experiences. But the future promises even more transformative change as AI adapts to students' emotional needs, motivating them during moments of frustration and celebrating their successes with genuine empathy.

Example 4: AI-Powered Adaptive Learning Platforms

Imagine an AI tutor that not only helps a student with their math problems but also detects when the student is becoming discouraged. The tutor then adjusts its feedback to offer positive reinforcement or a change in approach, improving both learning outcomes and emotional well-being. This is where the future of education is headed—toward personalized, emotionally supportive learning experiences that can adapt to each individual's emotional and intellectual needs.

Pro Tip: For educators, embracing AI's emotional capabilities could enhance not only academic outcomes but also foster a more supportive and empathetic learning environment for students.

5. The Balance of AI and Human Connection

One of the most profound questions we face as empathetic AI continues to evolve is: How will it impact the nature of human relationships? Will AI enhance human connection, or will it diminish the need for real human interaction? As we become increasingly reliant on machines for emotional support, we must be cautious not to lose sight of the irreplaceable value of human connection.

Example 5: AI in Relationship Coaching

There are already AI tools designed to offer advice and coaching for romantic relationships, such as *LoveBot*, which analyzes communication patterns and offers insights into improving relationships. While these tools are helpful in providing guidance, they cannot replace the depth and authenticity of human relationships. The future will likely involve a balance—AI tools that supplement our relationships but never replace them.

Pro Tip: As we integrate more AI into our emotional lives, we must ensure that it serves as a complement to, rather than a substitute for, genuine human connection.

6. The Responsibility of Developers: Building Empathy with Integrity

As we look ahead to the future of empathetic technology, one thing is clear: developers must take responsibility for ensuring that their creations are grounded in ethical principles. The power to influence human emotions through AI carries with it a significant responsibility to avoid misuse and exploitation.

Example 6: Developers Creating Ethical AI

Leading companies in AI development, such as *DeepMind* and *OpenAI*, have established ethical frameworks to guide their work. These frameworks ensure that AI systems are designed with fairness, accountability, and transparency in mind. For example, emotional AI should not be used to manipulate vulnerable individuals, but rather to enhance well-being in meaningful ways.

Pro Tip: Developers must prioritize ethical considerations as they build emotionally intelligent systems. By focusing on transparency and fairness, they can create technologies that serve the greater good and build trust with users.

7. Looking Ahead: The Role of Empathy in the Future of Technology

As we close this chapter and reflect on the road ahead, it's clear that AI will continue to play an ever-growing role in shaping human relationships. The ability of machines to recognize and respond to emotions is still in its infancy, but the possibilities are endless. The future of empathetic AI promises a world where emotional understanding is woven into the very fabric of our technology, helping us connect, grow, and thrive in ways we never thought possible.

Example 7: The Future of AI in Society

In the future, AI may be integrated into every aspect of our lives, from our personal relationships to our professional environments. Imagine a world where AI-powered companions are available to help us navigate the emotional complexities of daily life, providing guidance, support, and connection when we need it most.

Pro Tip: As we look to the future, it's important to remain mindful of how empathetic AI can be used to enhance our lives without over-relying on it. The true value of AI lies not in replacing human connection but in augmenting it in ways that promote emotional well-being and growth.

CONCLUSION: A Future Built on Connection and Empathy

The road ahead is filled with both incredible promise and deep responsibility. As AI continues to evolve, we have the power to shape its role in our lives. By focusing on the importance of empathy, ethics, and human connection, we can create a future where technology enhances, rather than diminishes, our relationships and our ability to connect with one another on a meaningful level.

Pro Tip: The future of empathetic AI will depend not only on technological advancements but also on our ability to balance innovation with compassion. Let's strive to create a world where technology enhances our emotional well-being and helps us build stronger, more meaningful connections with one another.

ACKNOWLEDGMENTS

I would like to extend my deepest gratitude to the many individuals who made this book possible. First and foremost, I thank my family and friends for their unwavering support and encouragement throughout this journey. Without their belief in me and this project, this book would not have come to fruition.

I also want to thank the researchers, innovators, and thought leaders in the field of AI, emotional intelligence, and ethics, whose work laid the foundation for this book. Their pioneering contributions to the development of empathetic technologies inspired me and provided the insights necessary to write these chapters.

A special thank you goes to the developers and engineers who continue to push the boundaries of artificial intelligence and emotional recognition. Their dedication to creating technologies that enhance human connection will shape the future of how we interact with machines and each other. I am privileged to have been able to learn from and build upon their work.

Lastly, I am incredibly grateful to my readers for their curiosity and passion. Your interest in how AI can shape empathy and human connection motivates me to keep exploring, writing, and sharing the latest advancements in this field.

Final Note: Share the Journey

If you found value in *The Empathy Machine: AI and the New Age of Connection*, I encourage you to share this book with others who might benefit from learning how artificial intelligence is reshaping our relationships, trust, and emotional connections. In an age where technology is evolving rapidly, we must understand the power it holds to transform our lives for the better.

If the insights and ideas presented in this book sparked new thoughts or deepened your understanding of the digital era, I'd be honored if you recommended it to your friends, colleagues, or social circles. Together, we can foster more meaningful conversations and build a world where empathy is at the core of technological advancement.

Please consider leaving a review or sharing your thoughts online—it not only helps me as an author but also inspires others to take part in this exciting journey toward a more empathetic future. Your feedback is invaluable, and I'm deeply grateful for your engagement with this book.

Thank you for being part of this adventure, and for helping spread the message of empathy in the digital world.

Michael Fink

www.ingramcontent.com/pod-product-compliance
Lightning Source LLC
LaVergne TN
LVHW051654050326
832903LV00032B/3805